Raw and Living Foods:
The First Divine Act and Requirement of a Holistic Living Way of Life

Raw & Living Fruits, Vegetables, Seeds & Nuts.
The Natural Foods for Man, He and She,
in the Divine Consumption Plan.

by High Priest Kwatamani

Kwatamani Holistic Institute
of Brain Body & Spiritual
Research & Dev., Inc.

MANIFESTING THE EXPRESSIONS OF
SUPREME LOVE, RIGHTEOUSNESS AND THE
HOLISTIC LIVING TRUTH ABOUT SUPREME LOVE

Edited by Queen Bea Kwatamani

This book is dedicated to the Supreme and Holy Spirit of the Divine Children of the Sun and their quest to achieve divine oneness with the Most Supreme Spirit of Love, Righteousness and the Holistic Living Truth About Supreme Love. There are no if's, no and's, no but's and no who's, because this book is dedicated to the Divine and Sacred Few.

TABLE OF CONTENTS

TABLE OF CONTENTS

INTRODUCTION: THE DIVINE CLARITY OF RAW AND LIVING FOODS: THE FIRST DIVINE ACT AND REQUIREMENT OF A HOLISTIC LIVING WAY OF LIFE

The subject of raw and living foods is a subject that cannot and must not be taken lightly at this point in time on the planet Earth. The state of being of the malnourished mind of thought is so clouded and so confused and so degenerated and so mutated that, unless there is an urgent and immediate switch—a complete change—to a holistic living lifestyle, the chaos and confusion of this spiritually disconnected and death-oriented mind of thought will completely annihilate the last vestige of the divine mental, physical and spiritual life force of all of those who participate in the consumption of dead and devitalized foods. Raw and living fruits, vegetables, seeds, nuts and grains are beyond a doubt the whole and natural nutritional consumption that the body craves and needs at this point in time of our existence upon the planet Earth. In fact, raw and living foods have always been the divine source of nourishment for the body, the mind of thought and of the spirit of Man, He and She.

The body of flesh has gone through such tremendous turmoil, misuse and abuse and has been inundated with such a massive overdose of toxic conflict and confusion that it is, in fact, in a state of total rebellion against the mind of thought's existing thought process. A thought process that upholds its consumption of dead and devitalized foods as a glorified way of life. Dead and devitalized foods that have been declared as normal and basic requirements by governments and social orders and institutions and educational facilities that declare mental, physical and spiritual aches and pains and deadly disorder as part and parcel of the intellectual state of being of "modern" man and "modern" woman within a "modern," "sophisticated" and "advanced" society. A modern society that prides itself on treating the vicious plagues of mental and physical illnesses as opposed to curing them. A modern society that instigates businesses and corporations that thrive on your mental, physical and spiritual illness and that provides pain relief as a priority. A society where whole healing, or even the talk of whole healing, is considered a rebellious and clandestine threat against the social economic structure of the status quo. A society where even the highest-paid and acclaimed participants become merciless victims of the mind maze while they pay a deadly cost to be the boss.

For example, medical doctors are considered as being one of the highest-paid professionals in America, yet they are one of the shortest lived. Isn't it amazing that, although medical doctors have such a short life expectancy, many people dream of joining this highly-touted profession? And just think, doctors are officially sanctioned as the caretakers for the massive mental and physical illnesses that are born from a devitalized and death-consuming way of life. In reviewing this analysis, it is blatantly clear that even with a greater social economic capacity to consume at the most highly desired and highest socially acclaimed nutritional level, the consequences of a dead and devitalized way of life consistently manage to find a way into their enzyme-depleted hearts, as well as their lungs, liver, colon and their malnourished brain cells, regardless of whether they are blond or bald or natty dread.

Wow! What an intellectual mind of thought! A mind of thought that has actually been reduced to intellectual insanity as a result of being reduced to intellectual consumption of dead and devitalized thoughts, dead and devitalized nutrients that, of course, will cause one to have and maintain an imprisoned spiritual essence. The essence of life, your whole life existence, your spirit, the divine and sacred gift of Love, the most supreme essence, the most supreme spiritual force field, your divine inner spiritual force field, the force field of Supreme Love, the essence of your sacred existence. The most supreme gift of Supreme Love, Righteousness and the Holistic Living Truth About Supreme Love, your sacred spirit. Yes, a sacred spirit that continues to be enslaved because of the dictates of a mutated and degenerated mind of thought. A mutated and degenerated mind of thought that is programmed not to refuse the taste of salted, sugared and otherwise seasoned dead and devitalized food substances.

The body is in rebellion. The body totally and absolutely rejects the whole concept and idea of consuming dead and devitalized foods. The body is in a total state of rebellion. A total rebellion against a mind of thought that has been viciously and deceitfully ingrained in the idea of consuming dead and devitalized foods as well as dead and devitalized thoughts that perpetuate dead and devitalized actions, attitudes, ways and behaviors; and social, political and religious values that perpetuate a culture of death. A culture of death worship, a culture of worshipping gods of death, a culture of worshipping the dead, a culture of worshipping yesterday, a culture that perpetuates the idea of a tomorrow and yet never faces the divine solutions, the divine evolutionary requirements and the divine necessities of today.

The body of flesh is in a rebellion, a rebellion that is so clearly defined at this point in time upon the planet Earth. The body of flesh is in a rebellion. The body is rebelling and its ways and means of rebelling are clearly signaled by the vast, massive disease that has inflicted Man, He and She's state of existence. A vicious and cruel state of diseased disorder that has never before been known upon this planet. Sure, there are all kinds of fast foods. Sure, there are all kinds of chemical drugs that have been taken to supplement and to substitute and to alter your existence. Sure, there are microwaves. Sure, there are pressure cookers. Sure, there are other processors—dehydrated-by-electric, nonsense consumption. Based upon values and misunderstandings about why you're upon this planet in the first place.

The body is rebelling. The rebellion is being signaled by heart attacks and cancer and diabetes and high blood pressure and low blood pressure and ulcers and colitis and birth defects and manic depression and psychosis and neurosis. The body is rebelling with chemotoma, incautoma and any other kind of name that we can create for the massive illnesses and mental and physical diseases that are plaguing Man, He and She, as a result of consuming dead and devitalized foods and thoughts and attitudes and behaviors. Nonsense consumption upon the planet Earth. The body is rebelling.

The body is rebelling against the very vicious kinds of depraved thoughts and behaviors that create such nonsense frames of thought that give signal and gratification and ok to ways that do not instigate and/or maintain your natural existence upon this planet. The body is rebelling through such consequences as AIDS. The body is rebelling by signaling some of the other kinds of venereal diseases that state very clearly that you must function with a sense of divine humility. That you must function with a sense of divine reality. That you must function with a sense of divine responsibility.

The body is rebelling with the manic kinds of depressed and depraved thoughts that cause people to bleach their skins and fry and perm and bleach their hair and alter their eyes and cut and pin and put chemicals and all kinds of ornaments all over their very precious body parts. Body parts that were created to reproduce themselves. Body parts that were created by the most divine and sacred Creator. Created by the most supreme Creator of life in order for us to go forward and multiply a more supreme creation of life.

The body is rebelling against death. And the consequence is a quick and painful state of living death for the mind of thought that is depraved and out of order with the wholesome life force of itself, the body and the spirit. The mind of thought has been disconnected from the spiritual essence. The body is rebelling against the mind of thought that instigates a suicidal thought process. The mind of thought that dictates the consumption of dead and devitalized foods. Dead and devitalized foods that create imbalanced chemical reactions inside the brain, causing all kinds of mental disorders. Mental disorders that give signals to the body of the pain and the pain that creates ulcerated conditions. The body is rebelling against the dead and devitalized food that does not provide the basic needs of life for the body, or for the mind of thought and fails to provide the supreme and sacred energy that is necessary to refuel the sacred and holy spiritual essence of life.

The body is rebelling against the consumption of dead and devitalized foods. The body is rebelling against any idea or thought that does not perpetuate the consumption of whole and live raw fruits, vegetables, seeds, nuts and grains in their whole and natural state of being. The body is rebelling against consuming anything other than the most supreme foods of the fruits of the trees of life, prepared and consumed in a live state. The body is rebelling against the consumption of the various liquids and liquors that do not provide whole life enzymes. The body is rebelling against drinking anything other than whole, natural fruit juices and vegetable juices. The body is rebelling permanently and that rebellion is causing an entire difference and change in the body's molecular structure.

The body is being degenerated and mutated, because one of the most primary necessities of the body is what is now presently called whole life enzymes—the factors of life that create the cell structures or refuel the cell structures or nourish the cell structures of the body's every single organ. Without these whole and live enzymes, the body has no possibilities of properly and divinely regenerating itself. Therefore, mutation sets in. Mutation, because the cell structures that are actually designed to reproduce themselves billions upon billions of times continuously have been reproduced in an out-of-order and degenerated state of being as a result of not being able to fully and wholly receive the divine enzyme nourishment that is necessary for natural and divine evolution. This occurs generation after generation after generation. And with each of these generations where it occurs, it breeds, into what is popularly called the DNA, a factor of mutation and degeneration. And those mutated and degenerated factors start to multiply themselves generation after generation. And the mutation continues until one has very little or no capacity to be able to reason divinely with common sense matters of fact. Matters of fact that directly relate to the fact that you must consume raw and living fruits, vegetables, seeds, nuts and grains in order to receive the full, whole, nourished divine factors that the divine, sacred and most supreme Creator of all life placed upon this earth to maintain you in a whole life state of being.

The body is rebelling against the idea that the brain has assumed the capacity to think and reason for the spirit when the brain is actually limited to its behind with only the ability to be programmed in an up-to-date manner—and only to be able to be programmed into fantasies and illusions about what tomorrow is while actually having no true idea of what is there before it. Thus far, creating an amazement, an amazed state of deceitful fear and fright about what is to be. A maze. A mind maze.

The body is rebelling against the idea that the brain is so fearfully frightened of the necessity and the idea of giving up dead and devitalized food substances. Dead and devitalized foods leading to dead and devitalized substance abuse which has caused a tremendous, habitual addiction to death. And the mind has been well-programmed generation after generation after generation. DNA mutation after DNA mutation after DNA mutation. Degeneration after degeneration. The brain has been reduced in its capacity to divinely reason and has very little capability of truly aligning itself with its most supreme inner essence, the most sacred spirit and, therefore, is lost and astray in a state of being of hopelessness. A hopelessness that's played out to the tune of a life that truly is a fantasy and an illusion of what one wishes it to be. Played out on the most vague ideas of love and love affairs. The most obnoxious ideas of communications and relationships, of consuming the most insidious frame of thought about the foods that are necessary for the body.

The mind of thought is in a tremendous state of trauma and the only way that that trauma can begin to be relieved is by a total, whole, dedicated state of living. A state of living where whole and live raw fruits, vegetables, seeds, nuts and grains become the total and absolute food consumption for generation after generation after generation until this divine regeneration leads Man, He and She, into a state of being where divine reasoning has taken its place upon this planet; and the war, conflict and confusion; the rape, the murder, the racism, the sexism; and the tribal, social, political and religious insanity will become a vanished mind of thought upon the planet Earth.

Therefore, the divine consumption of raw and living fruits, vegetables, seeds, nuts and grains is not only something that one must crave. It is something that is a basic need of life. The basic needs of life: living foods, sunshine and wholesome tender loving care. It is totally and absolutely impossible to have one without the other. The body and the mind are not capable of any kind of full, divine and sacred interaction, divine innercourse, or divine love affair—a basic need of life—if one is in a chaotic and confused and aching and painful state of being because of the unwholesome, dead and devitalized foods that have been consumed.

Love is most definitely supreme, but Supreme Love is not possible for anyone unless Supreme Love has been the divine consumption of that one. What you put in is what will come out of you and what will come out of you will draw back to you what you put in. If you put in death as dead and devitalized foods, you will put out dead and devitalized, mutated and degenerated thoughts, attitudes and behaviors that will subsequently perpetuate these dead and devitalized attitudinal thoughts and behaviors in your offspring through your DNA. The divine law is that what you put out will come back to you. You will draw back to you the personalities and the attitudes and the behaviors and the conditions and states of being of dead and devitalized thinking, attitudes and behaviors. Therefore, it is not possible to wholly receive the Supreme Spirit of Love, the Supreme Spirit of Love of the Most High, if one does not intake or put in the foods of the supreme spirit of Love of the Most High.

Very simple reasoning that is very, very, very complex for a depraved and devitalized mind of thought. Think about that as you read the materials in this blessed and sacred divine intervention of codes that are coming to you from the I in I of the most supreme spirit of the Most High.

FOREWORD

As excerpted from the August 18, 1999 Community Health Forum on Preventive Holistic Medicine   WCLK 91.9 FM, Atlanta, GA

The benefits of juicing and eating a live raw food diet

[Today] we're going to examine two major league secrets to great health, increased longevity, enhanced sexual performance, improved digestion, mental clarity and, most notably, how to greatly reduce your chance of contracting the current American epidemic of chronic degenerative disease. While the creation of health or disease has many causative factors, my experience as a medical doctor, healer and family man [has shown me that] juicing and eating a live foods diet can and will have a dramatic and positive effect on your health, happiness and effectiveness in life.... To digress for a brief moment, I must remind us ... of America's scoreboard on current, not so well publicized epidemics of chronic disease....   [Although] one trillion dollars ($1,000,000,000,000) [is] spent annually on healthcare, more than 50% of Americans develop heart and artery disease. ...And the other 50% basically of Americans develop cancer before reaching the age of 75. And increasingly, more and more and more Americans are becoming afflicted with arthritis, asthma, uterine fibroids,... Alzheimer's, diabetes, depression, digestive disorders, chronic fatigue, auto-immune problems, PMS, etc. and so on. The list of health ills in our society is virtually endless. ...I want you right now to know that juicing and eating a live foods raw diet are major steps to reclaiming our natural god-given health and longevity. Consider that humans and animals have evolved magnificently over millions of years without microwave ovens, electric ranges and crock pots. Our ancestors didn't have Campbell's soup, Kraft macaroni and cheese, Big Mac's and pasteurized milk on the menu. Judging from the fossil records, they also did not suffer from [the] physical deterioration or breakdowns that we experience on a processed, refined and cooked foods diet. Also consider that every living organism on the planet Earth is a 100% live, raw-foods eater. Not 99, not 70, not 50%, but 100%. However, there's only one organism that tampers with its food—human beings. We are the only animal on the planet that has decided to cook our food.

So, you might ask, why does the body function so much better on a fresh food diet? What does cooking and processing actually do to the nutritional value of food? First of all, heating beyond 110 to 120 degrees destroys the enzymes that all foods contain. These enzymes help us to predigest our food and thus avoid having to manufacture them. [When we eat cooked foods, because our body must now] manufactur[e] these enzymes, [we are] … robbing the body of energy and reducing our capability of manufacturing enzymes for other vital functions, including maintaining our immune system and fighting off cancer. Heating food destroys many vitamins that were originally present. Vitamins in the form of a pill are a poor substitute for the real thing. Heat processing reduces the oxygen that is available in fresh, live food that we need to resist disease with the oxygen. Many physicians now claim that cancer- and AIDS-causing viruses thrive in the low-oxygen levels in the blood and in the cells of people not in good health. Fresh food contains hydrogen peroxide which provides oxygen to kill these viruses. Eating heat-processed food triggers a massive release of white blood cells by our body, a similar response that happens when we have an infection or are poisoned. Fresh, uncooked foods do not cause such a reaction. While there's no consensus on why this occurs, it is clearly not a natural reaction and reduces our immune system's capacity to sustain optimum health when it is continually preoccupied with fighting off cooked and processed foods.

Now, we will also consider the fantastic world of juicing. Fresh fruit and vegetable juices [are] another priceless technique in maximizing our nutrition. The reason that the juicing of fresh vegetables and fruits is so effective lies in the fact that by separating [the] vitamin and mineral elements and the distilled water in the food from the fibers … a live liquid [is created] that is digested and assimilated in a matter of minutes and with little effort. On the other hand, to extract the same nutrition from vegetables and fruits by eating normally would require significant labor and time of our digestive process, actually hours, to be expended by our organs. Try drinking sixteen ounces of fresh carrot juice or eating seven large carrots. While the nutrition might be the same, it clearly would take more time and effort to eat the seven carrots than to drink the juice. Realize that the fiber [in] fruits and vegetables contain[s] no nourishment; however, fibers do serve a very useful and much needed purpose of acting as an intestinal broom. Therefore, fiber is important and we need an appropriate amount of good fiber in our regular dietary regimen unless you are juice fasting.

Many times, during a medical crisis, especially with chronic and degenerative illnesses, the patient experience[s] vitamin and mineral deficiencies as well as apparent [difficulty with] digestion and assimilation of food. Therefore, juicing is a quick, effective and efficient way to restore the body with much needed organic, vitamins, minerals and enzymes. Fresh juices are loaded with enzymes. Enzymes are the basic key of life present in our food that enable[s] us to digest food and absorb it into our blood. Enzymes act as an intangible, magnetic, cosmic energy of life which is intimately involved in the action and activity of every atom in the human body and every form of life. Enzymes are important catalysts which promote and stimulate good digestion, assimilation, cleansing and regeneration on a cellular level. Fresh juices are loaded with oxygen. Oxygen is one of the single most important elements that the human body needs to maintain health, especially on a cellular level and as soon as food is cooked, its oxygen is lost. Therefore, juicing is an effective form also of oxygenating our system besides exercise.

Juices are a liquid food, mostly organic distilled water of the finest quality with nourishing vitamins, minerals, oxygen, carb[ohydrate]s, proteins and enzymes that feed our bodies on a microscopic, cellular level. And that's usually where tissues are starved. …[I]t should be clear that our creator gave us food as both nourishment and medicine. Therefore, we can look at juicing as food and medicine. Finally, with this in mind, we trust it's clear that juicing can be a valuable and restorative technique that will nourish the cells and tissues of our bodies in the most speedy and efficient manner possible. So, in closing, if you're looking for increased energy and stamina, if you're looking for a solution to obesity, better skin and hair, health, how to avoid colds and flu, better digestion. If you're looking for increased sexual potency and increased longevity. And finally, if you're looking for ways to avoid major health concerns and avoid America's epidemic of chronic, degenerative diseases, I recommend that you incorporate into your life a more live, raw foods diet and live juicing....

Dr. William Emikola Richardson, M.D. and live foodist
Statistics researched and compiled by John Richardson

CHAPTER ONE:
THE CONSUMPTION OF DEAD AND DEVITALIZED FOODS: HISTORY AND CONSEQUENCE

Throughout the planet, the foods of death and devitalization have become the dominant foods of consumption. The Masters of Deceit who have forcibly taken social economic control of and dominate, the planet have perpetuated a religious philosophy and ideology that degrades the concept of stewardship, replacing it with the idea that to have dominion over the earth means to dominate, control, use, abuse and exploit every other form of life on the planet. This ideology of superiority infers that no other animal or form of life on the planet, other than humans, has any whole life value independent of its use and consumption value. The Deceit Masters have completely abused and misused the earth by polluting the air, the water and the soil. The animal and plant life of the planet is being tortured, slaughtered, boiled, stewed, baked, broiled, manufactured, processed, distributed, worn and consumed in a never-ending quest for profit and pleasure. The crux of this scavenger mentality is to use, destroy and discard.

The careless, ruthless and heartless perversion of the ideology of dominion has caused the entire population of the planet to be placed in extreme danger as a result of the pollution and misuse of the air, making it unsafe to breathe and leading to depletion of the ozone layer and global warming. The forests are being cut down, further disrupting the balance of the ecosystem by speeding up the rate of ozone depletion and destroying the natural habitat of thousands of life forms resulting in their eventual extinction. The cleared land is then used for the grazing of *live*stock who are enslaved and slaughtered for food and/or clothing. The soil is being stripped of its vital nutrients through over grazing and being further destroyed and contaminated by the garbage which is being dumped and buried underground and the pesticides and chemicals which are being sprayed upon the foods that grow from the soil. The earth is being robbed of its "precious" elements through strip mining, drilling, boring and other forms of extraction. Toxic waste, garbage and run off from livestock is being dumped and leaked into the water supply, contaminating it to such a degree that it cannot be safely consumed.

Thousands and thousands of animals have either become extinct or are being driven to extinction because of this ruthless exploitation mentality. For example, monkeys, mice and rabbits are injected with fatal illnesses, cut up and fed toxic chemicals all in the name of scientific advancement. Elephants and rhinos are hunted and killed for their tusks and horns and left to rot, so that individuals can have ornaments for their bodies or homes. Foxes, minks, snakes, tigers, leopards, bears and deer, and any other creature whose skin appears attractive based upon the values and tastes of the dominant society, are murdered so that their skins or their heads can be displayed like the trophies of war and bloodshed that they are. Even the adorable rabbit has been killed to be eaten, to be displayed as a coat and even for its feet—which are cut off and worn as "good luck charms," although, obviously, it is no good luck for the rabbit.

This "dominion" philosophy emerged from the Ice Age and its savage and scavenger behaviors of eating and sucking on the rot and stench of the dead flesh, blood and bones of animals and even other humans. As with animals, other life forms, the air, the water and the soil, this dominion philosophy extends to the social economic means of dealing with other human beings themselves, where, on the basis of race or color, some humans are considered to be superior to and have the right to control and use others. This mentality is exemplified by the invasions of ancient Kemet by its flesh-eating, cold-blooded and ruthless attackers as well as the invasions of the other ancient kingdoms of peace and love, such as China, which had to build a great wall to protect itself from its flesh-eating, cold-blooded and ruthless attackers. It is further exemplified by the the Islamic jihads and so-called holy wars against the Children of the Sun by their flesh-eating, cold-blooded and ruthless attackers; the slaughter and displacement of the Native American Children of the Sun by their flesh-eating, cold-blooded and ruthless attackers; the subsequent slaughter and virtual annihilation of the Australian aboriginal Children of the Sun by their flesh-eating, cold-blooded and ruthless attackers; and even the orchestrated and calculated genocide of a "lighter" breed of Children of the Sun called Jews in Nazi Germany by their flesh-eating, cold-blooded and ruthless attackers.

The quintessential example of this flesh-eating, cold-blooded and ruthless mentality is the North Atlantic Slave Trade, during the course of which well over 100 million "African" Children of the Sun were slaughtered or enslaved. Imagine slave ships that deliberately overcrowded and packed an excessive number of innocent, crying, screaming, squealing and mercy-seeking Children of the Sun on a ship so that they could be used as a live feast for the sharks to deter them from attacking the ship as it passed through the Northwest Passage. Imagine the entire act being practiced for so long that it became an enjoyable and entertaining sport-like adventure. Upon reaching the shores of the American continent, the surviving Children of the Sun were tortured, beaten, murdered, treated as chattel and used as free labor. After hundreds of years of building up the base and infrastructure of the current and dominant social economic system, the "African" Children of the Sun on the American continent and their descendants inherited a legacy of systematic racism and genocide as their greatest nightmare. That is to say, a post-slavery system of overt and covert racism, terror and genocidal practices was instituted in order to orchestrate their dismissal from the labor force and the social economic structure of America.

I'm sure that one or more of our readers is wondering what all of this has to do with live foods as the first divine act and requirement of a holistic living way of life or how it relates to this particular section on dead and devitalized foods. For the reader, I beg you to be patient and to ask yourself these questions: What was the diet of the orchestrators and their disciples and followers, of these vicious, cruel and barbaric acts? What was the diet that was being perpetuated by these vicious, cruel and barbaric orchestrators and their disciples and followers? And whether we like it or not, we also have to ask ourselves: What was the diet that was being consumed by the victims of these vicious, cruel and barbaric acts and is that diet still the consumption pattern that is continuing to keep them in a victim status?

What happens to the mind of thought, or "the brain," when a diet of dead and devitalized foods is consumed?

Let's get down to the basics here from the onset, so we know exactly where we are going. If you have a computer—that's something that we should all be familiar with—and the available current necessary to run it at 120 volts and you decide, as a result of a lack of understanding, that you are going to run it at 60 volts or less, the best that you will get is a dim light. And that dim light will only occur if the minimum requirement of 60 volts can turn it on. Let's forget the computer for now and deal with something else with which all of us are *not* so familiar, although we should be: the human body, its essence, the spirit and its thought-processing mechanism called the brain.

Let's take the thinking mechanism called the brain. Did you know that the brain requires more food nourishment than the rest of the body combined? Did you know that once the brain cells die, they cannot be replenished, unlike the cells of the rest of the body? Did you know that the higher the quality of whole food nourishment that is taken in by the body, the greater the whole food nourishment that is fed to the brain? Did you know that the greater the whole food nourishment fed to the brain, the longer the cell life expectancy and the greater the quality of thought and reasoning regarding whole life matters? Let's reverse that for a moment and see what the results are. Did you know that the greater the amount of dead foods taken in by the body, the greater the difficulty of the body to digest and eliminate that toxic waste from the body? Did you know that the greater the load of dead and devitalized food substances consumed, the quicker the body breaks down personally and genetically? Did you know that your body is in a constant state of war when the consumption of dead food occurs? Did you know that your defense immunity system has been specifically designed to seek, search and destroy any foreign or unidentifiable substance that enters the body? Did you know that only live enzymes are identifiable to the body's defense system and that any dead or devitalized substance immediately becomes an unidentifiable agent of war and therefore causes an immediate attack by the defense immunity system? Did you know that dead and devitalized foods not only cause a tremendous amount of stress and conflict within the body, but also cause dead and devitalized thoughts to manifest as a result of a malnourished brain?

Did you know that a scavenger diet creates a scavenger frame of thought? Did you know that a carnivorous blood-sucking diet, creates a carnivorous and blood-sucking frame of thought? Did you know that a diet that requires cold-blooded murder for the sake of fulfilling one's personal dietary satisfaction perpetuates a cold-blooded and merciless frame of thought? Did you know that football players and other vicious-oriented athletes are fed diets of death so as to perpetuate a killer instinct on the playing field? Did you know that toxins in the body create massive mental and physical irritation and that that irritation creates hostility, anger and overly aggressive behavior? Did you know that when training a dog, which is a carnivorous animal by nature, such similar measures are used to turn that dog into a hardened killer? Did you know that military training in preparation for acts of war, utilizes the exact same techniques to create a hardened and merciless killer-like behavior? And no matter whether it's a time of declared peace or war, the same killer instinct will be the signal of clear and present danger within any social environment encountered. Did you know that once these behaviors have been practiced and maintained consistently over long periods of time they will degenerate the genetic structure of the being consistently and eventually mutate the mental, physical and spiritual structure of the whole being into something completely opposite of what it once was? These viciously degenerative and murderously deceitful, mutated and mercilessly satanic behaviors are all a part and parcel of the norms of an adverse society that perpetuates a dead and devitalized diet.

Have we driven the point home completely yet, or do you feel as though we have gotten off of the subject? What was it that we were talking about? It definitely has to relate to the fact that you are what you eat and that your acts and behaviors are what you are regardless of who you say that you are. If this is clear to you, then it must also be clear to you, and it *will* also be very clear to you, that if you are a consumer of dead and devitalized foods, you are a consumer of death and deadly destruction. No matter how much you rap about spirituality and consciousness of mind and peace and love, in actuality, you are nothing but a New Age murderer by act or by consumption. Nothing more than a consumption-oriented murderer for the sake of greed, personal taste and sexual pleasure. Wait now. I wonder how that sexual pleasure snuck in there. Whoa! I guess that's because most of you, when you're setting your trap for your sexual opponent and prey, you normally use the flesh of some animal as the delicacy to lure the prey into your "love nest." You know what I mean? After you wine and dine him or her, he or she has got to give up the piece, baby. And as you know, a piece is an unwholesome consumption, because it is a part and not the whole. And it takes a sacred holistic living relationship to create the Spirit of Supreme Love, Righteousness and the Holistic Living Truth About Supreme Love. Just as it takes the Supreme Spirit of Love and Righteousness as a prerequisite to a holistic living relationship.

Focus on death instead of life

The consumption of dead foods actually leads to a mental and psychological preoccupation with death. The consumption of a death-oriented diet leads to death-oriented thoughts and behaviors. The mental focus turns from living and embracing life to preparing for death. Individuals pray to "God," seeking salvation from their earthly troubles and wait for a better life to come in the hereafter, when they will die and go to heaven to be with their god. They spend their entire lives praying, planning and waiting for that day. Individuals buy life insurance and put money aside to cover their burial expenses. They plan where they will be buried, next to whom and the details of the wording and design of their gravestones. Yet these same individuals will continue to consume dead and devitalized food substances, drink alcohol, smoke and engage in various other satanic and self-destructive behaviors, all the while praying to their god of mercy and wondering why they suffer from heart attacks, diabetes, high blood pressure, cancer or AIDS. These degenerative illnesses and diseases are the plagues that result from a death-oriented diet. These individuals never accept responsibility for the fact that they have created their own misery through the choices and decisions that they have made about how they live their lives. These individuals reject the basic requirements in life, the supreme will to consume divine foods: mentally, physically and spiritually.

Consequences of a diet of dead and devitalized foods

These death-oriented behaviors have social economic consequences as well. Mutated minds produce mutated and destructive acts and behaviors. Mutated minds also produce mutated offspring who will then reproduce mutated generations that have created and could even dwarf, today's present degenerative social ills such as crime, the growth of prison institutions, violent domestic relationships, degenerative diseases and various other forms of mental and physical illness. Perpetuating the concept of consuming dead and devitalized foods is a vital part of the capitalistic frame of reference. That is to say, the greater the massive consumption of these preserved and virtually useless food substances in jars and cans and what have you, the more convenient life appears to be and the greater the amount of time that can be utilized laboring for the proprietors, inheritors and benefactors of the social economic status quo. To earn a quick buck has become the modern convenience concept of those spending the bucks.

In actuality, a frame of thought has unfolded that states that the quicker and the more instant the better. A quick pill for headaches, instead of cleansing the colon and cleansing toxins from the body. Instant, microwave dinners which are kept "fresh" with morphine-like preservatives instead of eating fresh fruits and vegetables. Pasteurized juices, in which virtually all of the whole life value of the juice has been killed in the process, instead of taking the time to juice fresh fruits and vegetables. Chemotherapy as a quick hit, instead of taking the whole life measures to prevent the cancer in the first place or whole life measures to eliminate and replace the cancerous cells with live life cells. Insulin, instead of live juices, like string bean juice. Wearing of corrective lenses, instead of drinking whole, fresh carrot juice, wheatgrass juice, fresh bilberry juice and other live life herbs. In fact, the basic ideology is to eliminate the whole idea of divine spirituality and the idea of implementing whole life cures for the brain, body and spirit simply because it would cut out too many middle men and women.

The predominant societal attitude that we talked about earlier of "use, destroy and discard" extends to how individuals care for themselves, running themselves into the ground, eating and drinking anything. In an attempt to amass capitalistic security, whole life security of mental, physical and spiritual health is completely set aside. The replacement value is that automatic push buttons and remote control, vitamin supplements and drugs will create instant cures, although there are side effects. The basic concept is that there is no time for anything but working to earn as much cash value as possible before retirement, often dying before you have a chance to spend it. The most ridiculous and tragic part about the whole thing is that if individuals were living holistically and dealing with the real and whole thing in the first place, they would not have not have any need for the majority of the products that they are working so hard to consume.

A diet of dead and devitalized foods not only perpetuates mental, physical and spiritual illness for the consumer, but has an even more devastating impact on that individual's children. For example, an individual who may have eaten a semi-dead diet for a lengthy period of time and lived for a lengthy time has actually shortened the life span of his or her offspring by increasing the amount of his or her death consumption as a result of modernization, socialization and acceptance of a death-oriented diet and mental concepts as a norm. This is a massive and ongoing occurrence that can be viewed simply and easily generation after generation in the present societies that perpetuate a death-oriented diet. A person who may have had a heart attack at 80 will increase the chances of his or her offspring having a heart attack at 60. In turn, those offspring increase the chances of their children having a heart attack at 40. This pattern has been played out consistently generation after generation. You can see it within your own family group, with those close to you. You don't need scientific papers and documents to investigate this phenomena. Just look at your own family. You will see a clear statement of the genetic degeneration resulting from the massive consumption of dead and devitalized foods.

It is clear that the perpetrators and victims of these deadly behaviors cannot escape the consequences of their acts. The consequences of feasting on death and embracing the attitudes and behaviors of death can be easily witnessed: heart attacks, diabetes, emphysema, hypertension, cancer and various other forms of degenerative disease as well as other mental, physical and spiritual plagues. In fact, the various plagues that have amassed as a result of the consumption of dead and devitalized foods have virtually depleted the live life force of divine spirituality upon the planet Earth. This is basically because mass populations have been turned into obsessive death consumers, consuming death at such a rapid pace that no divine life force gets the opportunity of being reenergized. The end result is a downward spiral of destruction where insatiable greed and a total disregard for life inevitably cause depletion and devitalization which then feeds a more ruthless search to find and use up whatever life remains, resulting in further destruction. Thus, the survival of all life on the planet, including human life, is threatened, because the basic elements of life: air to breathe, water to drink and food to eat, have been polluted, contaminated and made unsafe to consume. It is clear that we are in a stage of Armageddon; it's just a matter of who or what will be the surviving life force. One thing is for sure. Death begets death, just as dead foods beget death and deadly destruction. Life begets life, just as live foods beget the live supreme love spirit of the Holistic Living Truth About Supreme Love.

CHAPTER 2: LOOKING FOR A DIVINE SOLUTION

Now that we have spoken quite clearly about the massive amount of problems that infest the planet Earth as a result of the consumption of dead and devitalized food substances, let us now begin to talk about ways and means of resolving these most fatal problems. Our approach is problem; solution. We first look at every aspect and detail of the problem so as to identify all of its most subtle parts from inception to birth and its present stage of infestation. For every problem, we must seek the solution to that particular problem first and foremost before going on to the next problem. We don't take a problem and add another to it to make two problems. Instead, we deal with one problem and one solution at a time. This enables us to encounter the next problem fresh, with the capacity for a solution. As the old kreo, West African saying goes, "You cannot dig a hole to cover a hole." Or if you dig a hole to cover a hole, you will always end up in the hole. The only way out of the death trap that has been described is to embrace life. The most basic means of demonstrating self-love, love for life and love for the Most High is through the consumption of live foods. Live, whole and natural foods in the raw: fruits, vegetables, seeds, nuts and grains.

The live foods diet is the first divine act and requirement of a holistic living way of life. What are live foods? A boa constrictor grabs a rat, poisons him and swallows him whole. A lion runs and catches his food and eats it on the spot, sometimes while it is still breathing. These creatures consume every single particle of their prey in a live state. They chew up blood, guts, bile, hair, eyeballs and bones all in one swallow. In each case, the foods being consumed are live foods, the live foods of a natural and short-lived carnivore. These are not the kind of live foods that we are talking about. Scavengers eat the remains of the dead. Some scavengers, like dogs, even eat human feces similar to some humans who eat hog or pig feces, or chitterlings as they call them. Clearly, this is not what we are talking about.

When we talk about live foods, we are talking about the natural foods for human consumption: whole, live and raw fruits, vegetables, seeds, nuts and grains without additives, preservatives, artificial flavors or colors. These are the foods of the Divine Children of the Sun. We are the gods and goddesses of the planet. We were given dominion over the Supreme Love Spirit of the earth. It is our responsibility to protect and preserve the Supreme Love Spirit of the earth and the wind and the rain and the sun. Therefore, it is our responsibility to maintain the best possible, wholesome, live foods for human consumption. The best possible, clean, wholesome air to breathe. The best possible, clean wholesome water with which to wash our external and internal systems. And live communication with the Supreme Love energy of the Sun. The body needs whole, live nourishment for optimal function and to produce whole, live thoughts, attitudes and behaviors.

In the introductory chapter, we addressed a single, but multi-faceted problem, *i.e.* dead and devitalized foods as a massively consumed substance that is causing the massive fatalities and life-wrecking illnesses that are spreading an Armageddon-like plague upon the planet Earth. In fact, the mind of thought that has generated from this dead and devitalized dietary pattern is threatening to ruin every life substance on the planet as a by-product of attitudes and behaviors which reflect no consciousness except to earn another dollar by any means necessary. When evaluating this particular problem, it becomes crystal clear that there is absolutely no repair possible for the structure of lies, lust and illusions, because it is so infested with the stench of death that any life form found hanging around would have to be transplanted into an entirely new life structure in order to survive. In fact, there is absolutely no room for live life structure, for live life living, or divine spirituality within the flaming foundation of the Masters of death consumption. Any attempt to forge a way into this rapidly deteriorating and collapsing structure would be a fatal step into mental, physical and spiritual suicide.

Oh!!! There are some games available within the structure of death consumption. Or should I say that there are some fads ready to happen at a moment's notice for those who have no better sense, will or desire than to buy into these fads of lies, lust, illusions and deadly destruction. There are fads like talking about free-range and organic flesh as a healthy alternative forgetting the fact that the murder of a creature is not justified by what it eats or how "humanely" it is murdered. There are games like preparing fried tofu, instead of fried chicken, games that cause one to ignore the fact that frying anything to death is dead. Although I'm sure that the chicken would be a whole lot happier with the idea that we are murdering the live life enzymes and numerous vitamin and protein factors of the soybean, instead of murdering Mr. or Ms. Chicken. In reality you wonder whether this is really a game to delay the consumption of Mr. or Ms. Chicken until the chicks have grown into full size several months later. I say that because that's about how long most of these fads last. There are games that address the idea of bean burgers instead of beef burgers, games that tell you that cooking food in winter environments keeps the body warm, when, in fact, what it really does is to cause the mouth a tremendous amount of heated pain and cause the body to go through massive fluctuations to try to maintain it's natural body temperature of approximately 98.6 degrees. There are even games that tell you to engage in live foods fasts while the ignorant forget the whole idea that eating anything and fasting is not synonymous. They are just not the same thing.

Please don't get me wrong. This social economic environment and its group participants, overseers and landlords have definitely got something for your confused death- and devitalized-consuming mind. This social environment has some people who have learned to ignore whole and natural reality placating themselves with fallacious ideologies that tell them that if they eat live foods once or twice a week and eat the foods of death and devitalization for the other five days of the week that they are of a more superior lifestyle. Then, of course, we have some of our favorite friends and so-called close relatives, declared as semi-vegetarians, fish-and-fowl vegetarians, ovo-lacto-vegetarians, macrobiotic vegetarians, vegan vegetarians and god knows how many other kinds and styles of dead-and-devitalized-food-consuming vegetarians. The rationale is that declaring oneself as a vegetarian consumer justifies the consumption of dead and devitalized food substances. Most of our vegetarian friends and so-called cousins, find it convenient to rationalize the consumption of dead and devitalized vegetables and what not as being a higher state of living and a more healthy and conscious state of being, because you are not taking the lives of the animals in the animal kingdom. However, what they are doing in reality is destroying the live life enzymes in the foods that they consume, thus destroying the live life electrical energy force of their own existence. What could be more fatal than instigating and participating in acts of self-destruction? Especially acts of self-destruction or depletion of your divine spirituality.

Let's keep in mind that life begets life, just as death begets death. And now, I hear that there is a new form of cooking where you cook a substance below 110 degrees as long as you wish. There are some mad scientists out there telling people that all of the life substance still remains in the food. This could be possible, especially if the solar rays were doing the cooking, but my question is who is sitting there with a thermometer while those beans cook for a half hour? In any event, let's not get into quaint details. Let us go right to the point at hand. We're talking the consumption of live foods as the first divine act and requirement of a holistic living way of life.

Live fruits, vegetables, seeds, nuts and grains: the natural foods for human consumption

What is the story about this live foods issue? Let's examine the mind of thought. I'm sure that right at this point in time, the mind of thought of many of our readers is questioning the ideas presented against these labeled vegetarianisms. If you think that that is something, imagine the reactionary possibilities from those who call themselves fruitarians. Right about now I'm sure some of you are beginning to get an understanding about which eating pattern is best for human consumption and you may also be beginning to feel the vibration as to why this divine Sun Child is so bent on exposing the fatal and destructive energy of the present-day dietary pattern including that of vegetarians as modernly defined by the deceit masters. As some of you are aware, the most widely practiced alternative dietary pattern is some form of vegetarianism. It is therefore a common and widely-accepted belief that a vegetarian diet is a better alternative than killing and consuming the flesh of dead animals.

The modern concepts about vegetarianism are that it is a superior way of eating for various reasons. The most common reason given is that, by consuming a vegetarian diet, the individual is not taking the life of an animal for food. Another common argument made in support of a vegetarian diet is that it has a less negative impact upon the Earth, because the unnatural concentration of animals in one place for breeding and slaughtering purposes has serious, detrimental environmental consequences. The waste/feces from the animals runs off into the water, contaminating the water supply. In addition, a widespread belief among vegetarians is that the raising of livestock leads to depletion of the ozone layer as a result of deforestation for grazing land and the large concentrations of methane gases emitted from the cows. Breeding and raising livestock uses large amounts of land, water and food. For example, the same quantity of water that is used to produce one pound of animal flesh could produce 100 pounds of wheat, while one acre can produce 1200 pounds of grain per year or 50 pounds of flesh. Finally, a vegetarian diet is seen as more humane, because the conditions under which animals are bred and raised. They are crammed into unnaturally small places, injected with hormones and fed completely unnatural and even cannibalistic, diets so as to produce as much flesh as possible as cheaply as possible. Vegan vegetarians feel even more justified in their behavior, because they do not consume milk products or chicken eggs and thus feel that they are not contributing to the enslavement of animals for their breast milk or for their young (eggs) which are taken and eaten.

It is not that these beliefs are not saturated with levels and degrees of truth, for I am very sure that these and many other valid principles must be upheld when consuming from this precious earth. However, when reviewing all of the above, there is one very supreme concept that has a greater degree of importance than all of the above. Let me clarify that. To exist upon this planet in peace, love and harmony is the most urgent necessity for those who were given dominion over all living things, the Divine Children of the Sun. With that in mind, it becomes imperative that the supreme self come into the supreme harmony of divine oneness with a wholesome and healthy brain, a wholesome and healthy body and a sacredly divine, wholesome and healthy spirit. In order for this to be accomplished, the very best, most wholesome, most complete and most natural forms of fuel must be fed to the body, the brain and the spirit. In this way, the supreme self is being given and being fed the supreme fuel of life and thus illuminating the Supreme Spirit of Love, Righteousness and the Holistic Living Truth About Supreme Love. I hope that you are following me here.

Let's take that last idea and expound on it. Let's start with the simple concept that "Good things start at home," and let's follow that one up with one just as simple: "You are what you eat." And then, let's add to that one a third concept that "What you put in is the sum total of what you put out and what you put out is the sum total of what will come back to you." Gee, I'm full of simple concepts today, huh? Wait now. Let's not take anything for granted, because there is definitely someone who is going to say, "What does this Divine Child of the Sun mean by that?" I've expounded enough. Let's get down to the nitty gritty of this issue by defining Supreme Love.

In order to define what Supreme Love is, the best approach is to define what it is not. Supreme Love is not putting your value judgments on some male or some female Sun Child or their offspring, declaring that, "I'd sure like to make love to her beautiful hips," which means that love can be unmade afterwards. It is not love to say, "I love Kentucky Fried Chicken." That's a hard pill to swallow since the chicken has been murdered and is thus incapable of reciprocating. Of course, you could be confessing to the fact that you love to murder other living things. If that's the case, I advise you to bear in mind the truth about consequences and that what you put out will come back to you in the name of "love" as you have expressed it. Without going very much further with the definition of love, it is my advice that henceforth you had better be very careful about the attitudes and actions you express in the name of love. Love is such a beautiful term and they say that there is a thin line between love and hate. Sounds to me like the Grand Master of Deceit was working on a new fad when they came up with that concept, because love is clearly bound and defined and has no opposite neighbors like hate hanging over a thin line. Anyway, we're not just talking about love here in and of itself. We're talking about the Supreme Spirit of Love. That is to say, the Supreme Righteousness of Love or, to put it bluntly, the Holistic Living Truth of Supreme Love.

Let's begin with the concept that good things start at home. Now, what do I mean by that? Pure and simple, what the I in I is saying is that your first priority in life; your primary responsibility; your sacred goal and objective, must be directed toward the supreme elevation of your innermost essence. Oh, that is "beautiful." Understand what I am saying here? To be frank, there is absolutely no need in walking around teaching, preaching, talking, rapping or lecturing about saving the world, or saving the poor people of the world, or saving the animals of the world or saving any life form on this Earth unless you immediately direct all divine actions toward the inner self, your most precious essence. Anything short of that is a con game or simply edification of verbal masturbation so as to better train to implement a con game.

Have you understood what I am saying here? What I am saying is that if each and every Child of the Sun on this planet and his or her offspring exercised his or her divinity by implementing the Supreme Spirit of Love for his or her most supreme essence, there would be nothing short of the Supreme Spirit of Love, Righteousness and the Holistic Living Truth About Supreme Love existing upon this glorious planet of ours. If you're following me, I have a question to ask you. Do you agree with me that the greatest gift that one can give upon this planet is to humbly yield to the Most Supreme Spirit of Love, Righteousness and the Holistic Living Truth About Supreme Love for the supreme inner self as a sacred entity of the *Most* High and Almighty God?? Now, only those who agree need to read further than this. For the rest of you, I suggest that you start over again after you have walked through various neighborhoods and the downtown center of your city or town and viewed the rampant murder, rape and suicide that is being broadcast on a daily basis over your television screen. For those of you who agree that the greatest gift that one can give to oneself is the Supreme Spirit of Love, Righteousness and the Holistic Living Truth About Supreme Love, let's move on to the second concept.

Okay, who's next? Ladies and gentlemen, now arriving in gate two is: You are what you eat. Okay, let's get ready now. This thing is getting deeper and deeper. Don't get lost in the melee of madness, because you know that there is a lot of b.s. out there. I'm sure you read above that they are stacking up a lot of cows and bulls in one location and what their waste is doing to the water supply and the ozone layer. Wow, there really is a lot of b.s. out there, both literally and figuratively. Okay, let's move away from the bad smells and get back to the concept that you are what you eat. I don't think we need to belabor this concept, but not taking anything for granted, let's re-expose this issue. If you eat dead foods, the live enzymes that would have normally existed within those foods are murdered through the cooking or the devitalization process. Once the live enzymes have been murdered, they are no longer available to that glorious mechanism within the body that distributes the live life force throughout the body system in order to maintain holistic living health. Added to that is the fact that the defense immunity system will immediately go on the war path against any unidentifiable substance that enters the body. We're talking about pure, unadulterated war, baby. Like it or not.

Therefore, let it be clearly understood that when you put that dead chicken, that dead cow, that dead pig, that dead fish, those dead beans, that dead flour, those dead vegetables or those dead fruit pies or what have you within the body system, you damn well had better be prepared for the consequences of that crime. Just to help you a bit, let me tell you some of the standard consequences of the standard crimes that are being implemented on the body each and every day. For example, for the crime of consuming white sugar, the punishment is sugar diabetes. For the crime of consuming processed salt, the punishment is high and low blood pressure. For the crime of eating flesh, the punishment is cancer. In fact, one in three of a specific group of Sons of the Sun is expected to contract prostate cancer by the time this book touches your hands. For the crime of consuming toxic drinks and fast, fatty and fried foods, the punishment is ulcers, heart attacks and obesity. For the crime of eating dead and devitalized vegetables, the punishment is malnourishment and emaciation. For the crime of smoking and breathing polluted air, the punishment is lung cancer. For the crime of drinking alcohol, the punishment is cirrhosis of the liver. For the crime of drinking animal milk, the punishment is lactose intolerance, the production of excessive mucous, ear infections and osteoporosis. Of course, all of these foods are major contributors to massive mental illnesses like manic depression and psychosis and are irritants which lead to laziness, suicide, hypertension, impotence, arthritis, rheumatism, aggressive sexual behaviors and destructive social behaviors like domestic violence, murder, theft and rape. Of course, these crimes create direct genetic mutation and degeneration of the brain, the body and the spirit as a major overall consequence.

Now what was it that I said earlier regarding truth or consequences? Whatever it was, it sounds like an introduction to this next concept. This next concept is something to be reckoned with. I advise that you look at every minute detail of this concept so as to be able to deprogram your brain and empower your spirit with the will to consume a live foods diet as the first divine act and requirement of a holistic living way of life. Okay. Last but not least, I now introduce a whole food for thought: The sum total of what you put in is a sum total of what will come out of you and the sum total of what will come out of you is the sum total of what will come back to you. Wow! That's deep!! Because according to this concept, if you are a consumer of dead foods in any degree, form, structure, or percentage, what will come out of you is the digested energy source, or non-energy source, of what you put in. And what you put out, affirmatively or negatively, based upon the substance that you put in to your mind, body and spirit, will be the bottom line as to what will come back to you. I want to say that again in another way. What this concept is saying is that when you eat dead and devitalized foods, it will produce dead and devitalized energies and an internal war of protection and the various consequences of destruction that come out of war. And that energy that comes out of you, no matter how subtle or how well disguised, will be, in part and in whole, the exact reciprocation of that which you put in.

Let me try it again. This concept is saying that if I eat live and whole foods, the holistic living foods of Supreme Love, Righteousness and the Holistic Living Truth About Supreme Love, the live and active enzymes and the whole vitamin and mineral resources of that food will generate positive and divine physical energy, positive and divine mental energy and positive and divine spiritual energy. As I put this divine mental energy out and this divine physical energy out and this divine spiritual energy out, the sacred and divine electrical energy source that I have tapped into will draw back to me the exact same sacred and divine mental, physical and spiritual energy that I have put out. This will tend to be reflected in my mind of thought and my mental health, in my whole body health and physical appearance and my divine and sacred spiritual stability. Therefore, I will be a reflection and would draw back that which I am reflecting in my every-day relationships on the planet. What I am saying is that life begets life, and the

Supreme Spirit of Love, Righteousness and the Holistic Living Truth About Supreme Love begets the Supreme Spirit of Love, Righteousness and the Holistic Living Truth About Supreme Love. Just as death begets death and the miserable consequences of lies, lust, illusions, confusion and deadly destruction.

For those who don't quite understand, or who wish to have further understanding of what I am saying, I will say it in a language that the majority can understand. If you eat dead and devitalized foods, regardless of the nature and degree of death and devitalization, the sum total of that dead and devitalized energy will be absolutely and completely the sum total of what will come out of you regardless of how you may attempt to edit it, modify it, sugar coat it or dress it up in fine print. The dead and devitalized energy, mental thoughts, the dead and devitalized physical degeneration and deterioration and the death and devitalization that will drown your spirit in the stench of death will be the sum total of what will come back to you. I hope you purely and absolutely understand what I'm saying.

When you have those sorrowful relationships that give you headaches and you can't understand why you keep drawing these kind of sorrowful and conflict-oriented personal relationships to you, the holistic living truth is that it began way back there with that piece of southern, fried death or that devitalized veggie burger. When you look at it, it happens time and time again; and you hear these individuals constantly saying over and over again that they are unlucky, or that they have just had bad experiences, or that they just can't get no satisfaction. What's strange is that it is hard for someone to recognize the fact that that innocent-appearing wining and dining on a meal of death and devitalization is in direct relation to the consequences that follow in the days after. The consequences come when you least expect it, or when you're least prepared or when you feel least able to honor them, or when you feel that you've gotten away clean. Consequences are real. Consequences are truth personified. Maybe that's why I refer to it as truth and consequences. Okay, so we've gotten that clear now.

I hope we understand now that it is totally not a relevant fact that you eat spinach every day. It is rather more relevant and vitally important that that fresh, organic spinach is not cooked or devitalized in any way or manner. It is not important to talk about how much broccoli, cauliflower, asparagus, kale, carrots, or other essential foods that you consume each day. It is rather more relevant and vitally important that you have consumed these commodities in their raw and natural state. As such, these divine foods are consumed either by whole, fresh and live juicing or whole, fresh and live mastication. To consume the divine foods of life in any other way is simply a major contradiction and a mental, physical and spiritual waste of time. For without whole life substance, any food, regardless of its organic state of being or its high vitamin/mineral or other essential trace element quality, will be of little or no value to your whole life system that we refer to as the body.

Let's make this simple. When your body receives whole foods, your entire cell structure puts out a welcome mat. Your defense system dances with joy and jubilation and the live, life enzymes of your body immediately mate up in divine oneness and marriage with the live, life enzymes of any whole, live and natural foods that you consume. In this way, the whole and live and natural fruits, vegetables, seeds, nuts or grains that you have consumed become the vital part of your divine essence and in actuality become the sum total of who you are—divinely, lively and naturally. That's right ladies and gentlemen, that's what I'm telling you: You are what you eat. If you eat a fresh, live and whole apple, you become the sum total of the life force of that sweet, juicy fruit. By the same token, if you are consuming any of the dead beasts of prey, or the devitalized and illy-prepared vegetables or fruits, your whole life energy will become that of a dead ankh. A dead, rotten and deteriorated fish or a dead freshly-killed creature. Either way it does not matter, your energy will become infested with the juices of murder and deadly destruction, because you are what you eat. It doesn't matter whether you created that first fresh kill or whether you bought it from the supermarket, you are either a cold-blooded murderer by act or a cold-blooded murderer by perpetuating the consumption of the life force that was slaughtered in an act of viciously-justified murder. It isn't so bad that you are what you eat. More importantly, the holistic living fact remains that you must bear the consequences for the death that you eat or the divine life consequences for the life that you eat, or should I say, for that other divine life energy force that you merge with in your holy temple.

For some very sacred and divine reason, I sincerely feel that you, you who have the ears to hear and the spirit to feel and direct the divine will, now understand that there is no better way to express the Supreme Spirit of Love, Righteousness and the Holistic Living Truth About Supreme Love other than through a whole, live foods diet. A diet that consists of whole and natural fruits, vegetables, seeds, nuts and grains—the whole and natural foods for human consumption. We who have the ears to hear and who recognize that we are of the Divine and Sacred Few have heard, felt, sensed and understood the supreme necessity for a whole, live and natural diet of the holy foods of the Trees of Life.

Again we say, the divine and sacred foods for human consumption are unequivocally live fruits, vegetables, seeds, nuts and grains, unprocessed, uncooked, un-pasteurized, without additives, preservatives, or artificial flavors, or colors. It is my hope that all we need to discuss at this point in time is the best and most appropriate way of integrating a live foods diet into your sacred existence; however, before we do that it is necessary for us to find divine clarity from lust, lies, illusions and commercial-oriented confusion.

Therefore, in the next chapter, we are going to present to you an organized analysis of the vitamins and minerals and other essential elements that are classically identified as necessary for whole health. We will follow that by discussing the essential whole foods and point out their nutritional and healing properties. We are extremely sure that the classically identified food nutrients are a mere scratch on the surface of what whole and live foods provide for the body. Although we acknowledge these classically-identified vitamins and minerals, we also acknowledge that the whole foods of fruits, vegetables, seeds, nuts and grains are the only perfect foods for divine human consumption. Therefore, any identified item that is not found in whole foods is definitely not necessary for human consumption. There are thousands of food substances which scientists have yet to identify or understand, but one thing is definitely understood: it takes whole and live, fruits, vegetables, seeds, nuts and grains that are power-packed with whole and live enzymes to assimilate with the whole and live enzymes of the body in order to nourish and rejuvenate the divine life cell structures of the holy temple of the body and the brain. When this holistic unification of divine live foods occurs, it brings the body and the brain to an apex under the direction of the most supreme and holy spirit. As the Most High would have it, divine oneness of the supreme essence of life takes place. In the spirit of the Most High, the Most Supreme and Holy Spirit of Love, Righteousness and the Holistic Living Truth About Supreme Love, please allow divine clarity to come forward within this body of flesh, this mind of thought and the essence of the holistic living spirit within.

CHAPTER 3:
DIVINE CLARITY REGARDING LIVE FOODS AS THE FIRST DIVINE ACT AND REQUIREMENT OF A HOLISTIC LIVING WAY OF LIFE

And the vegetables shall be your medicine and the fruits shall be your meats and you shall dwell in the house of the lord forever. Wow! Something that I just said is a clear and obvious indication that life begets life forever. Hmmm! And it seems something else there said that one of the reasons that there is so much confusion, conflict, lies, lust, illusions and deadly destruction is because dead and devitalized foods beget dead and devitalized attitudes and behaviors. It makes one understand why there is a direct parallel between the fact that live, whole fruits, vegetables, seeds, nuts and grains were replaced by dead and devitalized foods and this replacement factor has therefore caused mass conflict, confusion and deadly destruction upon the planet Earth. It is quite apparent that consuming dead and devitalized foods automatically, in and of itself, voids your existence in the house of the lord forever. It automatically prevents your rites of passage into divine oneness with the Most High, the Most Supreme and Holy Spirit of Love, Righteousness and the Holistic Living Truth About Supreme Love. In actuality, the consumption of dead and devitalized foods creates an automatic void and vacuum between your mind and your spirit, therefore cutting you off from divine knowledge, divine wisdom and divine understanding.

Live and whole fruits, vegetables, seeds, nuts and grains: the natural foods for human consumption. The most supremely sacred and precious foods of the Divine Children of the Sun. Wow! Have we really gotten off track on this planet! Oh, excuse me! No, not we. That's definitely not the case. That's the misuse of a subject pronoun, because we, personally, have corrected our problem with a divine solution. Let's rephrase that. Wow! Have things and those who support the insidious madness and fatal destruction of wild and satanic frames of thought, really gotten out of hand on this planet! Problem. That is a serious problem. This is a serious problem. Ladies and gentlemen, we have a serious problem upon the planet Earth. A problem that must be addressed urgently and immediately without a moment to waste. A problem that has manifested a satanic and Armageddon-like plague that is spreading deadly and fatally-painful diseases like wildfire. Diseases that we all know very well: cancer, heart attacks, diabetes, hypertension, psychosis, neurosis and other mental illnesses and AIDS, to name a few. Dying disease. Diet disease. Dying diet diseases that totally and absolutely ignore whole life food substances as natural preventive medicine and the natural cure for the body.

It seems as if it is done by design. When you really analyze it, it seems as though somebody, or a group of somebodies, are systematically orchestrating attitudes and behaviors that will forge a greater dependence on supplements, pills, injections, hospitalization, prisons and mental institutions. It sounds like the "New World Order" of capitalism is deeply invested in pharmaceutical industries, prison institutions and the manufacture of artificially-produced and preserved food substances. Sounds like a deeply invested problem. Or a problem that has been deeply invested in and heavily financed. A problem that has become an absolute norm within social economic environments that house the sickest, most hostile and most reactionary individuals upon this planet.

Problem. Solution. I don't know about you, but as for the I in I, I've long since had enough of this problem. So, if you don't mind, I wish to take you deeper into the inner zone of a holistic living way of life. A way of life that perpetuates the divinity of nature. A way of life that perpetuates your supreme union and divine oneness with the Most Supreme Spirit of nature and the universe. A way of life that perpetuates the Most Supreme Spirit of Love, Righteousness and the Holistic Living Truth About Supreme Love. A way of life of live, whole, natural fruits, vegetables, seeds, nuts and grains: the natural foods for human consumption. Oh! Did I not tell you that the only way that you can pass through the gates of divine oneness and union with the Most High is to surrender your holistic living will to your most supreme essence? I also need to remind you that life begets life and it takes whole, natural, live fuel to supply your supreme temple with the kind and type of divine energy force necessary to achieve supreme oneness between the I, or your spiritual essence and the Most High.

Let's not get ahead of the situation or take anything for granted. Let's not get ahead of ourselves or our precious readers who will definitely have some socially programmed concerns about rejecting dead and devitalized foods for the sake of consuming the divine and live foods: fruits, vegetables, seeds, nuts and grains. First, let's address some of the vital needs that the body has, as presently identified and accepted within the social, economic structure that is now dominating the planet Earth. Below, in the following pages, we shall take the time to list for you some vital information that will directly relate to the present day mindset of wholesome food consumption. Please bear in mind that the Holistic Living Truth About Supreme Love will clearly indicate that live fruits, vegetables, seeds, nuts and grains are the divine foods for human consumption and, in and of themselves and properly combined, they are completely capable of providing every possible live, life nutrient that your body needs and requires. They are the most wholesome and most natural and most divine foods that exist on the planet Earth for the consumption of the Divine Children of the Sun and their offspring.

Until you have researched the problem, you have not the right to speak about it. After you have thoroughly reviewed and analyzed the following nutritional information, it is our hope that you will have reached divine clarity and that your greatest concern will be to find the quickest, most expedient, urgent and effective means of getting these foods into your whole life system so as to get you activated in living by the sacred principles of Supreme Love, Righteousness and the Holistic Living Truth About Supreme Love. Please take your time and we'll be back with you later.

Classical data regarding a balanced diet

The massive lies and social-economic-oriented deceit that has been taught to us and those who came before us is that we need to eat a certain number of servings of flesh, dairy products and cooked grains and vegetables, in order to be healthy. We are told that we should eat three square meals of this kind a day and two snacks. The deceit that has been perpetuated is that a balanced and healthy meal would be something like dead flesh as the main course; cooked and devitalized grains and tubers like bread, rice and potatoes as side dishes; with cooked, canned or devitalized vegetables as side dishes; and canned or cooked fruit for dessert. We are taught that we need the flesh of a murdered chicken, cow, pig, or fish for protein. We are taught that in order to get sufficient calcium, we need the breast milk of cows and goats or milk byproducts like cheese and yogurt, although this milk was intended for growing a baby calf into a quarter of a ton animal or a baby goat into a miniature-sized cousin.

It is quite apparent from the massive amount of mental and physical illness perpetuated throughout the modern Westernized environment and the environments of its disguised and associated kin, that something has gone extremely wrong throughout this era of deceit. There should be absolutely no question that the sum total of what you put in is the sum total of what will come out and the sum total of the energy that comes out of you will be the sum total of the energy that you draw back to you. Please don't forget that you are what you eat. And you are a sum total of your acts and *not* your sugar-coated words. So, there it is America. The holistic living truth about a dead and devitalized diet.

Love it, or leave it. As for your body of flesh, mind of thought and that sacred spirit that has been so massively depleted, what I have to say regarding your food consumption and your whole life body: Change it, or lose it totally and completely to a fate of death and deadly destruction.

Exploration of lies and alibis

Let's begin with the idea that we need dead flesh for protein. Let's compare a 100 mg. serving of broiled lean, ground beef with a 100 mg. serving of raw spinach. Approximately 40% of the calories in that beef come from protein. The remaining 60% come from saturated fat and cholesterol. With the spinach, 46% of the calories come from protein, approximately 10% from unsaturated fat and the remainder from carbohydrates. The spinach has zero cholesterol and zero saturated fat. Clearly, you get more protein per calorie from the spinach without the artery clogging, prostate cancer causing saturated fat. Well, that idea that you need beef for protein died with the cow. Maybe we can still save the meal. Let's explore the other deceit-oriented idea that you need beef for iron. According to the USDA, per 100 calories of beef, there is 1.1 mg. of iron as compared to 11.3 mg. of iron in a 100 calorie serving of spinach. Oh well, there goes dead flesh down the drain. That must be the reason why cows prefer to eat green leafy vegetables instead of another cow, or a fish, pig, or chicken.

What about milk and all those deceitful, exploitative and self-serving advertisements that say that milk does a body good or that milk has something for everybody. We need milk for calcium, right? A 100 mg. serving of spinach has 81 mg. of calcium and that form of calcium is available for human or animal consumption and is capable of naturally maintaining and enhancing the genetic structure of any creature that eats it. The calcium contained in the cow's milk is inorganic and in a form which cannot be used by the body. The DNA factors in cow's milk are specifically designed to produce a quarter ton creature in the same way that the DNA factors in a human mother's milk are specifically designed to create a human being. Any conflict between the DNA factors of what is consumed and the individual consuming will automatically produce conflict and confusion in the mental, physical and spiritual development of that individual.

So, there you have it again. Milk definitely has something for everybody depending on which body mass or type and kind of species that that milk is coming from and going into. I guess that that advertisement was fool proof and safe from legal claims of false advertising, because goat milk has something for goats. Opossum milk has something for opossums. Cow milk has something for cows. And human milk has something for humans. For those who are planning to feed their children breast milk for their health and longevity, most obviously, a human child should be consuming human breast milk, unless you're trying to raise a human cow. Of course, when you look around in today's modern and advanced American society, you see a lot of human cows running around mooing and chewing their cud. Anyway, here's a little added information as food for thought. Human milk contains 5% of its calories from protein, the amount of protein necessary for a human child to properly grow and develop. It takes 180 days for a human baby to double its body weight. In comparison cow's and goat's milk contain 15% and 17% of their calories from protein, respectively, and it takes 47 days and 19 days respectively for a baby calf or goat to double its birth weight. You can imagine the impact that the consumption of this kind of milk has on human beings. It builds huge, big boned, heavy cow-like individuals.

Analysis of essential vitamins and minerals as classically identified

Protein/Amino Acids

Amino acids are found primarily in proteins and are needed by the body for digestion and tissue growth, maintenance and repair. Amino acids are key in regulating the metabolism, the hormones and the blood-sugar levels and are necessary for proper nerve function and for fighting infection. High protein live foods include: pignola nuts, pumpkin and squash seeds, wheat germ, peanuts, sunflower seeds, almonds and sesame seeds.

Carbohydrates

Carbohydrates are the body's primary energy source. Once eaten, they are converted to glucose which is then used by the body for energy. Insufficient carbohydrate intake interferes with the metabolism and causes fatigue. High carbohydrate foods include all fruits, especially bananas; grains, and fresh corn from the stalk.

Fats

Fats are needed by the body for concentrated energy and to create fatty tissue within the body. This fatty tissue helps to regulate the body temperature and acts as a protective cushion for the nerves and muscles. Essential fatty acids are needed for healthy skin, proper hormone function (including the sex hormones), proper nerve function and proper brain function. A deficiency of essential fatty acids can lead to severe skin rashes, emaciation, retarded growth, high blood pressure, heart disease, PMS, menstrual difficulties, sterility and infertility. Good sources of fats include nuts, seeds, avocados, coconuts and pure extra virgin olive oil.

Vitamins

Vitamin A

Vitamin A is necessary for maintaining the tissues that line the external and internal body surfaces. It is necessary for good eyesight, strong bones, healthy skin, hair, teeth and gums, a healthy gastrointestinal tract and proper immune function. Deficiency results in dry, rough skin and pustules on the skin and scalp, poor bone and teeth formation in children, tooth decay, vision problems, digestive problems, the inability to gain weight and kidney and bladder infections and disorders. Deficiency can also lead to muscular degeneration, including degeneration of the muscles of the heart and infections of the ear, nose, mouth and respiratory system. Some foods with high concentrations of Vitamin A are carrots, corn off of the cob, sweet potatoes, winter squash, broccoli, lettuce, cabbage, leafy green vegetables like spinach, kale, (sweet) potato greens, collard greens; dandelion, turnip, mustard and beet greens; watercress, parsley, apricots, oranges, cantaloupes, mangoes, papaya, peaches, prunes, watermelon, pecans and peppers.

Vitamin B$_1$ (Thiamine)

Vitamin B$_1$ is necessary for proper metabolism of carbohydrates, proper nerve function and is essential for reproductive function. Deficiency causes low energy, muscle weakness, nervous problems such as irritability, mental depression and insomnia, loss of appetite, craving for sweets, low blood pressure, slow pulse, confusion and poor memory. Good sources of Vitamin B$_1$ are barley, millet, rye, wheat and other grains; almonds, brazil nuts, hazel nuts, pecans, pine nuts, walnuts and other nuts, peanuts, cashews and other seeds, leafy green vegetables like collards, mustard greens and kale; mushrooms, broccoli, cauliflower, asparagus, corn, coconuts, apricots, avocado, raisins and pineapple.

Vitamin B$_2$ (Riboflavin)

Vitamin B$_2$ is necessary for healthy skin, hair and eyes; for the proper assimilation of iron and proteins and aids in the breakdown of carbohydrates. Deficiency leads to poor vision, including cataracts; rough, cracked and scaling skin; poor appetite, weight loss, swollen tongue and ear infection. Sources include asparagus, broccoli, carrots, lettuce, cabbage, okra, spinach; collard, turnip, beet, dandelion and other leafy greens; watercress, apples, avocados, blueberries, prunes, grapefruits, lemons, almonds, cashews, mushrooms, pumpkin and sunflower seeds.

Vitamin B$_3$ (Niacin)

Vitamin B$_3$ is necessary for proper conversion of carbohydrates into energy, as well as aiding in the digestion of fats and proteins. Deficiency can lead to skin diseases, inflammation of the mucous membranes and intestines and ulcerated lesions on the tongue, cheeks, lips, rectum and anus and the vagina; mental depression accompanied by irritability, suspicion and hostility, fear, confusion, insomnia, dizziness, headaches, nervousness and loss of appetite, weight and strength. Good food sources are peanuts, millet, wheat, barley, asparagus, broccoli, collard greens, kale, turnip greens, potatoes, tomatoes, almonds, avocados, bananas, cantaloupe, dates, figs and mushrooms.

Vitamin B$_5$ (Pantothenic Acid)

Vitamin B$_5$ is necessary for proper functioning of the digestive system, adrenal function, maintenance of healthy muscle tissue and growth. It is good for fighting stress, fatigue, nervous disorders and infection. Deficiency can lead to prematurely gray hair, rheumatoid arthritis, digestive problems, rough skin, mental depression, infertility and birth defects. Sources include cantaloupe, broccoli, cabbage, carrots, cauliflower, mushrooms, spinach and other green leafy vegetables, sweet potatoes, wheat and other grains, peanuts and walnuts.

Vitamin B_6 (Pyridoxine)

Vitamin B_6 is necessary for healthy teeth, proper functioning of the pancreas, maintaining muscle tone and has a soothing effect on the nerves. It aids in proper protein, fat and carbohydrate metabolism. Deficiency can cause anemia, insomnia, fatigue, irritability, depression, decreased appetite, poor digestion, deterioration of the mucous membranes, ulcers and lesions on the skin, mouth and throat, clogged arteries, nausea and diabetes. Sources include cabbage, mushrooms and green leafy vegetables, grains, bananas, blueberries, cantaloupe, raisins, avocados and nuts.

Vitamin B_{12} (Cobalamin)

Vitamin B_{12} is necessary for proper red blood cell formation, including the proper functioning of the blood-forming organs of the bone marrow and for proper nerve function. Deficiency results in anemia and nervous degeneration. Other symptoms include insufficient production of the sex hormones, leading to shriveling or lack of development of the breasts, ovaries and sex organs and irregular menstruation or cessation of menstruation. Sources include sea vegetables and sprouts.

Biotin

Biotin is necessary for metabolism of proteins and fats and for proper immune function. Deficiency can cause skin disorders, anemia, lethargy, depression, insomnia, hair loss, muscle pain, poor growth, nausea and loss of appetite. Sources include almonds, walnuts, banana, raisins, raspberries, grapefruit, mushrooms, tomatoes and whole grains.

Choline

Choline is necessary for proper liver function, metabolism of fats and proteins and for proper nerve function. Deficiency results in poor growth, water retention, cardiovascular problems and hemorrhages in the kidneys, heart muscles and adrenal glands. Sources include leafy green vegetables, vegetable oils, seeds, nuts and grains.

Folic Acid (Folacin)

Folic acid is necessary for healthy blood formation, enzyme efficiency, the division and growth of new cells and for maintaining a healthy intestinal tract. Deficiency can lead to birth defects, anemia and digestive problems. Sources include dark green leafy vegetables such as spinach, watercress, mustard greens, beet greens and turnip greens; parsley, carrots, mushrooms, asparagus, beets, broccoli, sprouts, root vegetables, grains and cantaloupe and other fruits.

Inositol

Inositol aids in the metabolism of fats. It is good for regulating hormone function and controlling cholesterol. Deficiency causes poor liver function, diabetes and hair loss. Sources include citrus fruits, sprouts, leafy green vegetables, zucchini, tomatoes, wheat, oats, nuts, almonds, peanuts and other seeds and onions.

PABA

PABA is necessary for maintaining the reproductive glands and organs, maintaining natural hair color, fighting bacteria and for protection from sunburn and other burns. Sources include wheat, asparagus, broccoli, sprouts, root vegetables and dark green leafy vegetables.

Vitamin C

Vitamin C is necessary for maintaining the supporting tissues of the body including cartilage, bones, teeth and connective tissue. It is necessary for the production of collagen, which holds cells in formation and helps to fight infection. Signs of deficiency include bleeding gums, tendency to bruise easily, excessive bleeding from minor cuts, slow healing of wounds and fractures, anemia, poor bone and cartilage formation and susceptibility to infection. Sources include acerola cherries, green and red peppers, guava, asparagus, cabbage, leafy green vegetables, watercress, horseradish, broccoli, cauliflower, potatoes, mangoes, cantaloupe, papaya, kiwi, tomatoes and citrus fruits.

Vitamin D

Vitamin D is necessary for normal development of teeth and bones. It is synthesized in the skin by sunlight. Signs of deficiency include rickets, nearsightedness, soft teeth, muscle cramps and tics, slow healing, insomnia and nosebleeds. The best source of this vitamin is from sunlight.

Vitamin E

Vitamin E is necessary for maintenance of normal red blood cells, proper functioning of the reproductive organs and the metabolization of fats. It aids in proper immune function and helps to prevent blood clots and heart disease. Deficiency can result in infertility, deterioration of the nervous system—nervousness, irritability, headaches and fatigue; slow growth and defective development of the reproductive cells; and, in women, habitual miscarriage, absence of menstruation, late maturing and infrequent ovulation. Vitamin E is found in plant oils, whole grains like barley, rye and wheat; asparagus, broccoli, cabbage, corn off the cob, parsnips, sprouts, lettuce, leafy green vegetables, apples, strawberries, cherries, sunflower seeds, almonds, walnuts and other nuts.

Vitamin K

Vitamin K is necessary for proper blood clotting. Deficiency can result in hemorrhages and excessive bleeding. It is good for protecting against bone loss and cirrhosis and jaundice of the liver. Good sources include alfalfa, leafy green vegetables, cruciferous vegetables, sprouts, sea vegetables, oats, wheat and rye.

Minerals

Calcium

Calcium is necessary for healthy formation of the teeth and bones. It is also necessary for building muscle, wound healing and coagulation of the blood—therefore preventing excessive bleeding and proper metabolism. Deficiency results in brittle teeth and bones, osteoporosis, weak muscles (including the heart muscle) and poor growth and circulation. Calcium can be found abundantly in sea vegetables, leafy green vegetables and sesame seeds. Other good sources include broccoli, sundried figs, dates, raisins, sunflower seeds and celery.

Chlorine

Chlorine is necessary for healthy joint and tendon operation. It helps to prevent gum disease (pyorrhea) and stimulates liver activity and digestion. Deficiency results in excessive accumulation of waste matter in the body, resulting in self-poisoning or auto-intoxication. Sources are sea vegetables, alfalfa, beets, celery, cabbage, carrots, onion, parsnips, tomatoes, endive, lettuce and green leafy vegetables like spinach, dandelion greens and watercress.

Chromium

Chromium is necessary for glucose tolerance and sugar regulation within the body. Deficiency can lead to poor carbohydrate and fat metabolism, high cholesterol, heart trouble, diabetes and hypoglycemia. Sources include apples, grapes, raisins, green leafy vegetables, mushrooms, nuts and whole grains like wheat and rye.

Copper

Copper is necessary for iron absorption, protein metabolism, bone formation and blood formation and clotting. Deficiency results in anemia, weaknesses, heart arrhythmia, nervous conditions and poor resistance to disease. It is found in avocado, cauliflower, almonds, walnuts and other nuts, millet, raisins and grains.

Fluorine

Fluorine increases bone density, fights infection and reduces the incidence of tooth decay. Deficiency may cause tooth decay, poor eyesight and susceptibility to infection. Sources include cauliflower, cabbage, cucumbers, sea vegetables, spinach and other green leafy vegetables.

Iodine

Iodine is necessary for good thyroid function as well as proper regulation of the glands. Iodine is necessary for healthy skin, hair and nails and proper wound healing. It protects the body from toxins and aids in metabolism. Deficiency leads to thyroid disorders, menstrual difficulties and confused thinking. Sources include sea vegetables, grapes, cranberries, oranges, pineapples, asparagus, green leafy vegetables, mushrooms, cabbage, celery, carrots, cucumbers and lettuce.

Iron

Iron is necessary for building the red blood cells and distributing oxygen throughout the blood system. It is necessary for a strong immune system and for proper healing from injury. Deficiency results in anemia, muscle weakness, lowered resistance to disease and fatigue. Sources include cherries, sun dried apricots, sun dried peaches, prunes, raisins, blackberries, black raspberries, pineapple, grapes, leafy green vegetables, sea vegetables, asparagus, cauliflower, beets, sweet potatoes, winter squash, millet, almonds, pumpkin seeds, sunflower seeds and wheat and other grains.

Magnesium

Magnesium is necessary for good nerve and muscle function. It promotes sleep, is good for an overall sense of wellbeing and is good for the complexion. Magnesium also aids in tooth and bone formation and heart and kidney health. Deficiency results in emotional instability, depression and muscle spasms. Sources include sundried apricots, banana, cherries, pineapple, raisins, raspberries, strawberries, cantaloupe, prunes, avocado, sea vegetables, broccoli, fresh picked corn, beets, cauliflower, dark green leafy vegetables such as dandelion greens and spinach; almonds, walnuts and other nuts, peanuts, pumpkin seeds, barley, oats and other grains.

Manganese

Manganese is necessary for activating enzymes as well as other minerals within the body and for proper sex hormone production. It aids in immune response and sugar and fat metabolism. Deficiency results in poor hair and nail growth, loss of hearing, poor muscle/joint coordination, blindness and deafness in infants and sterility. Sources include apples, apricots, bananas, pineapple, asparagus, beets, celery, broccoli, carrots, leafy green vegetables such as spinach; parsley, lettuce, squash, sea vegetables, almonds, nuts and grains.

Phosphorus

Phosphorus is necessary for nourishment of the brain and growth of the bones, teeth and hair. Deficiency can result in mental fatigue, poor bone development and depression. Sources include almonds, sesame seeds, pumpkin seeds, nuts, oats, wheat, rye, broccoli, green leafy vegetables-especially kale and collard greens, fresh picked corn, prunes and sea vegetables.

Potassium

Potassium converts carbohydrates into energy and stimulates the liver. It is necessary for proper muscle function, heart health, nerve stability and enzyme and hormone production. It aids in healing and maintaining the body's chemical balance. Deficiency can result in liver ailments, muscle paralysis, constipation and water retention. Sources include bananas, dates, cantaloupe, papaya, peaches, raisins and other sun dried fruits, asparagus, cabbage, carrots, garlic, onion, winter squash, avocado, potatoes, spinach, tomatoes, sunflower and other seeds, grains and sea vegetables.

Selenium

Selenium works with Vitamin E to prevent fat and cholesterol accumulation in the blood. It enhances skin and body tissue elasticity. Selenium strengthens immune function and protects the body from environmental and other toxins. Deficiency leads to skin and liver damage, digestive cancer and hypothyroid condition. Sources include asparagus, broccoli, cabbage, mushrooms, kelp, sesame seeds, garlic, onion, wheat and other grains.

Silicon

Silicon is necessary for growth and health of the body's connective tissue. It is necessary for healthy bones, tendons, ligaments, cartilage, skin, hair and nails.

Deficiency can cause baldness, gray hair, skin problems, tooth decay and poor vision. Sources include apples, grapes, figs, strawberries, asparagus, beets, celery, cabbage, parsnips, green leafy vegetables, tomatoes, spinach, lettuce, barley and oats.

Sodium

Sodium is necessary for regulating kidney and body fluid function. It is necessary for proper iron absorption and aids in digestion. Deficiency can result in iron deficiency, indigestion and the formation of calcium deposits around the bones and joints leading to arthritis and rheumatism. In addition, deficiency can cause gallbladder and kidney stones. Sources include cucumbers, strawberries, beets, carrots, celery, okra, pumpkin, turnips, spinach, beet greens, dandelion greens, watercress and other green leafy vegetables; string beans, sea vegetables and wheat.

Sulfur

Sulfur is necessary for proper liver function and protein absorption. It gives one smooth skin, glossy hair and hard nails. Deficiency results in impurities in the blood due to inhibited liver function. Sources include sea vegetables, onion, garlic, hot peppers, horseradish and mustard, asparagus, green leafy vegetables, watercress, cauliflower, broccoli, cucumber, turnips and fresh picked corn.

Zinc

Zinc is necessary for proper immune function, mental alertness, gland health and sexual and reproductive health. Deficiency can lead to mental disorders, birth defects, depressed immune function and reproductive disorders. Sources include mushrooms, pumpkin seeds, onions, nuts, sunflower seeds, spinach and wheat.

Enzymes and raw and living foods

I have been asked whether there is a connection between enzymes and DNA. Enzymes are necessary for the proper functioning of each and every living cell within the body. Enzymes are also necessary for the proper reproduction of DNA. DNA is the genetic blueprint for all living things that is contained within the living cells of the body. What happens when the body is deprived of live-life enzymes? Body and cell functions break down, a process of cell deterioration and degeneration. Likewise, the process of DNA and cell reproduction breaks down. Because of a lack of live-life enzymes, the body's DNA cannot properly replicate and reproduce itself, resulting in deterioration, degeneration and mutation of the genetic structure of the individual. This genetic deterioration, degeneration and mutation manifests in the form of sickness and diseases such as hypertension, diabetes, cancer, ulcers, colitis, manic depression, psychosis and neurosis. Degenerated and mutated DNA is passed on from one generation to the next. Each successive generation has a greater likelihood of suffering from sickness and disease and of having a shorter life expectancy. The eventual results of the continued consumption of dead and devitalized and enzyme-depleted foods are death, disease, degeneration and genetic mutation. The only way for the body to enjoy whole mental, physical and spiritual health and well-being is through the consumption of raw and living fruits, vegetables, seeds, nuts and grains—the only foods in which live-life enzymes are found in their divine and natural order.

The positive or the negative reality regarding the DNA is that the blueprint that your foreparents have is inherited by you through the cell shell of your birth. When the negative norms of the status quo are applied, the degeneration continues at a very rapid pace. Generation after generation after generation continues to pass on the DNA handicaps, and the only way you can advance positive regeneration of your cell structure, your DNA, is through the progressive and aggressive intake of raw and living foods, *i.e.* raw and living fruits, vegetables, seeds, nuts and grains—the wholly and divine foods for the consumption of Man, He and She.

Just as this degeneration and regeneration affects the body in clear and obvious ways and means, it affects the brain and your thought processes to a greater degree. I say to a greater degree, because the brain cells do not replenish themselves, and they require whole life nourishment in order to thrive and generate accelerated and divine life thought processes. Therefore, when I say you are a sum total of what you have consumed mentally, physically and spiritually, it should be very clear from a physical perspective that what you consume will affect the mental perspective of how you think, act and behave.

Another thing to note is that when the organs of the body are in their proper and divine order, they require less energy to function which in turn creates a greater supply of energy to be used in the thought process. The brain thus has a greater supply of energy and is thus able to handle a greater demand of thoughts, reasoning and analysis. This enables the brain to be able to take what appears to be complex thoughts and reason them into simple and common-sense understanding, therefore giving a person the ability to come up with simple solutions and divine-oriented resolutions. Therefore, holistic living consumption is important, because the brain actually requires more nourishment than the rest of the body in any state of being. When consuming dead and devitalized foods, not only are you robbing the body of essential and extremely necessary energy sources, but you are also instigating a malnourished brain which feeds a malnourished mind of thought.

So when we say a person is a sum total of what he or she consumes, it should be clearly understood that when you consume dead and devitalized foods, you have no other choice but to produce dead and devitalized thoughts which will foster dead and devitalized relationships from dead and devitalized frames of reference. By the same token, when you consume live-life foods, it will eventually correct your degenerated and mutated cells by correcting the DNA in your cells and will cause the progressive healing of the body and, most importantly, divine enhancement of the spirit within, your life-force, allowing you to go forward and multiply more wholesome and healthy generations that are yet to be born.

On so many occasions, during well over a generation of the I in I consuming raw and living foods and working with others to develop and maintain the raw and living way of consuming, I have witnessed many a personality begin to transform into a being of a much higher consciousness of mind and a much more naturally-defined way of behaving. I have had many individuals testify to the I in I that something very profound is going on in their life, that they are totally in awe over the consciousness of sight and simplicity of reasoning that is beginning to emerge into their life. So many continue to testify that they cannot believe the amazing state of mental, physical and spiritual health and well-being, and the greatest wonder in their life stimulates from the fact that they have an amazingly different sight to see things that surround them that they've never before seen, although looking from the same eyes. I have to admit that consuming raw and living fruits, vegetables, seeds, nuts and grains and maintaining a holistic living way of life will have a tremendous impact on your relationships and associations with others, especially if they are the consumers of dead and devitalized foods. We advise you to seek out a divine social economic family community or strong support units of that kind, because you will definitely have a change of mind.

CHAPTER 4: SOME GENERAL NOTES ABOUT SHOPPING

When shopping look for every organic fruit or vegetable that you can find. Make very sure that you respect the divine energy of life, and do not shop in an area where dead creatures are kept. Because the spirit of those who are buying flesh and those who are keeping it will interrupt the spirit of the whole fruits, vegetables, seeds, nuts and grains that are being purchased. In addition, the negative aromas of death will interrupt your whole system.

Make sure that you purchase ripe fruits. For marketing purposes, many of the marketers have fruits picked green so that they will have a longer shelf life. Often, these foods are picked before they are ripe, therefore, losing their wholesome natural flavor and nutritional content. Avoid picking fruits that are green, bruised, cracked or open, discolored or hard. For example, I have witnessed people buying avocados that were hard which did not ripen for two weeks or that rotted before they ripened. I've also witnessed this with peaches and bananas that are picked too soon. They can rot before they ever ripen.

When picking green leafy vegetables, pick the young leaves. The primary reason why the young leaves or vegetables must be picked is because of their tenderness and because they are easier to digest or assimilate. The older leaves are an indication of the seeding process. When the leaves of foods like cucumber begin to turn yellow after they have grown massively or flowers have started to grow on them, that particular vegetable or fruit has aged or matured to the stage where it is preparing to bear seeds to re-fruit itself. Although these vegetables can be consumed if necessary, your best quality and taste will be acquired when they're picked in their early stages of maturity.

Be very careful of wilting leaves or of wilting vegetables or fruits. That's an indication that they're not fresh and have been on the shelf or in the bins too long. With fruits like watermelon or other melons, look for the coloration. The coloration will tell you something about the ripeness of that melon. Make sure it is not too light. This shows that the melon was picked too early and is not sweet. It is also necessary to plunk the belly of the melon. When you get a drumbeat sound, that is an indication that the melon is fresh and juicy as opposed to dry and mushy. When a melon sits in the sun too long off of the stem, it becomes dry.

A note on condiments

Generally speaking, these are not part of a living foods diet and should be avoided. However, there are a few products that we use that are holistic.

Sun evaporated sea water: Use in moderation. Use only without additives or preservatives.

Raw, organic apple cider vinegar: Raw, organic apple cider vinegar may be used for pickling and marinating vegetables. It is highly nutritious, made from whole organic apples and has a completely different biochemical makeup than other vinegars. White distilled vinegar or wine vinegars contain a harmful acid which attacks the body system by destroying red blood corpuscles and interferes with the digestive process. It is also a contributing factor in causing cirrhosis of the liver and ulcers. On the other hand, raw apple cider vinegar contains an acid which works with the body system to produce energy and aids in the building of red blood cells and the coagulation of blood and is thus effective in cases of excessive bleeding from nosebleeds, hemorrhoids and during menstruation. Raw apple cider vinegar has also been used to treat varicose veins. It is high in potassium and a natural antiseptic. It helps to balance the system and aids in the digestion of proteins. If the product says raw and does not say organic, that is a sign that it was made with apples that contain chemicals, were sprayed or otherwise. Be assured that these chemicals will interfere with the life elements of the vinegar as well as the life elements of those who intake it. Hain's raw, organic apple cider vinegar has been a product that I have used for a very long time over the years when I have not produced my own. However, there are several other good brands on the market such as Spectrum and Braggs.

Nama® Shoyu: Nama® Shoyu is a raw, unpasteurized soy sauce. It is full of live enzymes and beneficial organisms like lactobacillus. It is made from whole soybeans, whole wheat, sea salt and koji. We recommend Ohsawa® brand. They use organic ingredients and age the soy sauce for four years in cedar wood kegs. It is a good source of sodium and contains no additives, preservatives, artificial flavors, or colors. Please be aware that any food with living enzymes in it will continue to develop. Therefore, Nama® Shoyu should be stored in a cool, dry place in order to prevent fermentation. Please see appendix for communications from our distributors, to be shared with the students and guests of the Institute, regarding a shipment of Nama® Shoyu that we received.

Extra virgin olive oil: When purchasing olive oil, buy first cold-pressed, extra virgin. The preference is for a stone-ground oil, such as Bariani, a California company. Stone grinding produces little or no unnatural heat and, therefore, will ensure the life enzyme quality of the olive oil. When extra virgin olive oil has not been accessible to the I in I, the substitute has been fresh, home-made nut oils such as coconut oil or, when in Africa, palm nut oil. Let me make it clear that we are not talking about cooked oils!

Position of Divine Clarity

Recently, I have heard some concerns expressed regarding the use of nama shoyu, although the product is labeled as raw. It has been my experience that Ohsawa® brand Nama® Shoyu is the best product of its kind that is available on the market. It is labeled certified organic and is labeled raw.

However, it is my position as the spiritual leader of the Kwatamani Holistic Living Family Community that the best and most wholesome practice is to use products and ingredients that are easily identified as whole foods, i.e. raw and living fruits, vegetables, seeds, nuts and grains and that are readily accessible to you from the land and/or from the sea. Keep in mind that favorite seasonings of the I in I are sea kelp and sea dulse and, of course, celery. We also use sun evaporated sea water and Celtic sun evaporated sea water.

Please note that in all of the recipes in this book, sea kelp, sun evaporated sea water or Celtic sun evaporated sea water can be smoothly substituted or exchanged. Remember that it is the fresh herbs that give you the ultimate taste, and that is what we use to bring you that well-defined Kwatamani flavor.

Over the years, I have had the opportunity to participate in the creation of raw nama shoyu and other kinds of products that stimulate the common taste bud. The creation process is one that takes time and care to properly age and ferment the product. One should always be aware that there are ever-present commercial incentives to speed up processing time which always lead to a dilution in product quality and nutrition, as well as tricks of language where a "raw" label does not necessarily mean raw and living.

For those of us who are concerned with divine consumption, we must actively begin to support product manufacturers who produce products that are uncooked, unpasteurized, unadulterated and unfiltered and be prepared to stand by this position. Keep your eyes open for a line of products coming soon out of the Kwatamani Veganic Gardens and Spiritual Retreat™. Be aware, however, that any Kwatamani product will have a very short shelf life. Therefore, they will be best found and enjoyed on-site.

CHAPTER 5: SOME GUIDELINES ON WHEN AND HOW TO EAT

As should now be clear, the holy foods are raw (uncooked) and unprocessed, live fruits, vegetables, seeds, nuts and grains. Only in its raw and natural state can foods be properly and completely processed and assimilated by the body.

- At the beginning of the day, after sleep, your body is breaking a fast. During the time while you sleep, you are fasting. After waking, the first meal consumed will break the fast. Break-fast should be sensitive to the rest and cleansing that the fast provided to your body. You should not consume anything heavy at this time. Instead, *the first thing that you should consume is fresh-squeezed/fresh-pressed fruit juice.* This is what your body needs at this time of day and what is easiest on the digestive system. The juice lubricates your system and allows it to function optimally. Fruit juice is best, because fruits are easier for your body to digest than vegetables. And fruit juice is best in the early day, because it gives that burst of energy that the body needs, quicker and easier, for a system that has been shut down through the night. Fruits, as compared to vegetables, are higher in the energy food substances that we identify as natural sugars.

Note: Canned and bottled juices are not fresh. Many of them have been pasteurized (subjected to extreme heat), diluted, reconstituted and/or have had additives, artificial colors, artificial flavors and preservatives added. They are completely devoid of the digestive enzymes that are vital to your body. Therefore, let's make it very clear that we are talking about fresh squeezed/fresh pressed live and whole fruit juices.

Fresh fruit juices and fresh vegetable juices are meals in and of themselves and one of the quickest and most expedient means of consuming the whole nutrients that the body needs. When consuming fruit or vegetable juices, the juices should linger in the mouth so as to mix the saliva with the whole food content of the juice. This allows for better and more expedient digestion/assimilation of the live life enzymes in the food.

- Your first meal should be fresh fruit. Fruits are best eaten alone, but can be combined with raw, unprocessed and unsalted nuts. (See guidelines below regarding food combining). Fruits cleanse the body by flushing it of toxins. Wait at least 10-15 minutes after drinking your juice before eating.

- Prior to eating any meal, including your afternoon/evening meal, you should drink juice. Vegetable juice is best before your afternoon/evening meal. It signals to the body that you are about to change from fruit to vegetable consumption. Vegetable juices are best consumed before a vegetable meal.

- Your late afternoon/evening meal, taken closer to bedtime, should be a vegetable meal. Vegetables take longer to digest than fruits. This meal can be a combination of grains and vegetables or nuts and vegetables. All vegetables can be eaten in their natural and raw state.

- You can eat as much as you want as long as you follow the above pattern. You can maintain any healthy weight with a live foods diet that you wish. It simply depends on the combination of foods that you eat.

- You may snack as often as you like. Whole, live fresh fruits as well as sun dried fruits and dried nuts make good snacks. It is extremely important that any dried fruit or nut have enough mastication time so that the saliva can aid in digestion. It is a good idea to soak dried fruits or nuts in live whole fruit juices like apple juice in order to aid in the digestive process. Avoid eating dried nuts and dried fruits together. This is a difficult combination for the body to handle, because all of the liquid content in the foods has been removed, making it necessary for the body to provide much needed liquid content.

A Few Words about Food Combining

The purpose of proper food combining is to not overburden the system with too many different kinds of foods at one time that may or may not be easily digested together. At all times, it is important that foods be eaten and prepared for maximum digestibility. The classical rules about food combining follow with our own observations:

Fruits

Fruits are generally classified into three categories: acid fruits, sub acid fruits and sweet fruits.

Acid fruits include:
Citrus fruits, sour fruits and berries, kiwi, pomegranates, pineapples, strawberries, tomatoes, limes and lemons.

Sweet fruits include:
Bananas, persimmons, carob, figs, dates, papaya and dried fruits.

Sub-acid fruits include:
Apples, peaches, sweet cherries, berries, guava, pears, mangos, plums, apricots and grapes.

- As a general rule sub-acid fruits are said to best be eaten with either acid fruits or sweet fruits, but not both in the same meal.

- Sweet fruits also combine well with predigested or soaked nuts and seeds. Sub-acid fruits can also be eaten with predigested or soaked nuts and their milks, spreads and sauces.

- It is very important not to mix watermelons, or any melon, with any other fruits. Melons are best eaten alone or combined with other melons.

- Citrus fruits should be consumed together for best results. However, we've found orange banana juice to be an excellent combination that my body has said bring more to. Besides that, on our plantation in West Africa, the bananas and the oranges grow right next to each other and are often eaten in the same meal. However, I do find eating an orange by itself to be a more acceptable assimilation of that fruit.

- Our approach to the consumption of fruits is based primarily on the concept that fruits that are grown in the same vicinity are most likely able to be consumed together without severe digestive problems. *e.g.* Avocado and banana can be eaten together and also produce a tremendous taste. During my past twenty years of living in a tropical environment of Africa and the prior years spent in Asia, what I have learned is that the food combining concept is best suited when tropical fruits are consumed with tropical fruits. For example, such fruits as banana, pineapple, coconut, orange, sugarcane and mango are most likely to be able to be combined in some manner. However, I find it best to consume the whole fruit in and of itself. I also find it very necessary that nuts be consumed with fruits and that seeds be consumed with the fruits that they are seeding.

- As a general rule, avoid combining vegetables and fruits in the same meal, except: a) although avocados, tomatoes, cucumbers, lemons and limes are fruits, because of their low sugar content, they can be eaten easily with vegetables. In other words, avoid combining fruits that are high in sugar with green vegetables. b) lettuce can be combined with fruits.

- My experiences have shown me that grapes, for example, are an excellent combination with grape leaves. When I've examined the nutritional value of grape leaves, I have found them to be similar in nutritional value to dark green leafy vegetables like spinach. Thus, when I've had the occasion of having grapes without grape leaves, I have found the combination of spinach with grapes an excellent way of consuming these green leaves. My initial experience in relating the combination of fruits and the leaves came from my observation of gorillas and other monkeys, but most especially, the gorillas. I've noticed that in the wild when they're consuming their fruits, they seem to habitually pull a few leaves to eat with the fruit for whole nourishment. Therefore, I do not find it safe to say that fruits should not be eaten with green leafy vegetables. Bananas do not have any green leaves as we would know them, as I result I've never found it necessary or advisable to eat bananas and green leafy vegetables together. Bananas tend to combine best with high protein/fat foods, like nuts and avocados.

Vegetables

- Vegetables combine best with other vegetables or with either nuts/proteins or grains/starches.

- What I have found is that cabbage and cauliflower should not be eaten in the same meal, unless you don't mind producing a lot of gas.

Seeds, Nuts and Grains

- Avoid combining nuts, seeds, avocados, olives, seed and bean sprouts and other high protein foods in the same meal with grains. Also, it is best not to combine several proteins in the same meal. The Kwatamani live foods diet eliminates starch completely. The body produces its own starch. We find it contradictory to consume any starchy foods. Even with fresh corn, a delicacy of the family, we only eat it in its freshest and youngest state where it is easily digestible sugar. Once it sits, it becomes starchy.

- Avoid combining grains and fruits in the same meal, although soaked/sprouted grains can be combined with sweet fruits, like oatmeal with bananas and dates. Grains are best eaten with vegetables.

Seeds go best with vegetables; however, seeds can be combined with fruits. What I am saying here is that fruits have seeds and to get the full nourishment out of that seed, it is best to consume the fruit with that seed if you are going eat the seeds. All of the creatures that I have witnessed, including myself and my family, consume the seed of the fruit with the fruit, only saving a few to be replanted. As a matter of fact, we have found many seeds to be extremely delicious, especially when combined with their fruit. For example, we have found olive seeds to be very delicious. We find almond seeds to be very delicious, especially with their fruit. Oh! I forgot, almonds have been declared as a nut. I guess the people who were declaring food categories did not know that almonds were a seed to a fruit.

I understand that fruits and nuts are said not to be a good combination. What I would say about that is that nuts also go very well with vegetables. I would also say, the wetter the nut, the better the digestive process, either through mastication or the soaking process. I find dates and nuts to be an excellent combination. I also find bananas and nuts like almonds and brazil nuts, tropical nuts, to be an excellent combination. I find that pistachios are better consumed with green leafy vegetables. I've basically found that bananas and apples have the ability to be consumed with most other nuts.

Avocados and nuts are a poor combination and will certainly cause a lot of gas as a result of the high protein content of the combination.

A Word about Grains

When consuming grains, it should be noted and well-understood that a grain like corn (which can be viewed as a seed, a grain or a vegetable), wheat, etc. is at its nutritional best and at its highest sugar content when consumed fresh. (For a nutritional breakdown on corn, please see page 87). Anything short of that will find the sugar of that grain turning into a starch. Be aware that the body has the capacity to produce its own starch. Please note that the body converts the sugar it consumes into a starch. When the body intakes the sugar and utilizes it for energy, the by-product of this process is starch which is used for secondary energy burn. The primary energy for all body activities is sugar. This divine and natural whole sugar can only be found in raw and living fruits, vegetables, seeds, nuts and grains—live and in living color, with fruits being your primary energy source.

Be aware that what the commercial processing companies do is to "deactivate the enzymes" in various products such as rolled oats so as to maintain the shelf life. In deactivating the enzymes, one does just that, depleting the life in the foods resulting in a loss of vital nutrients. Although the shelf life of the grain has been extended, the whole nutritional life—the most valuable living-life substance of this shelf product, is lost forever in a maze of commercial and consumer jargon. It should be noted that it is nothing but commercial and consumer jargon that identifies a product as "organic" when the life substance has been cooked out of it during its processing. It has been clearly shown that the commercializers have come to understand the ignorance of the consumer when it comes to labels, for it is only in a deep state of ignorance that an individual would have any concern whether a product is organic or not when the most essential life substance of that product has been depleted in order to maintain shelf life. After all, the whole purpose for consuming the product in the first place is for its living and life-giving essence. If you have any doubt about this phenomenon, just take a trip to your local health food store. There you might miss the small fresh produce section hidden amongst the aisles and aisles of processed, bagged, boxed and canned organic corn chips, organic baked beans, organic tofu, organic candy, organic supplements and other dead products with other organic dead substances included. There seems to be little concern about consuming all of these dead and devitalized food substances, because they're *organic!* I wouldn't be surprised if they have organic liquid smoke to be used for barbecuing, just like they have organic flesh of a dead animal—justifying the consumption of death through the use of terminology like organic and free-range.

A Word on Eating and Drinking

Wait a minimum of 30 minutes after eating fruit before drinking or eating vegetables, although a longer period would be better.

Wait 45 minutes to one hour after consuming vegetables before consuming juice. Clearly, it is advisable that the vegetables be left to digest through the evening/night. However, if you have some urgent need for juices, this waiting period should be honored.

A Word about Water

Water is an excellent cleanser, but it is not a nutrient. One should drink it as one wills. It is highly advisable that large quantities of fruit and vegetable juices be consumed. This will provide you with organic water as well as the vital nutrients that the body needs and deserves. In the end, your body will put that liquid out as urine anyway. The most nutritious water that one can take to drink is not distilled water. It is not spring water. It is coconut water. Coconut water is full of the divine electrical forces that are used to balance the body system. It is also very nutritious and acts a natural cleanser for the whole body system. (See the next chapter for more information regarding the benefits of coconuts and coconut water).

CHAPTER 6:
LIVE FOODS: FRUITS, VEGETABLES, SEEDS, NUTS, GRAINS, HERBS AND SPICES

Please review each of the following foods carefully. Take time to review their health benefits and characteristics and the type and kind of nutritional traits available in each of them. We shall begin with the fruits, listing each fruit and its identified nutritional traits and health benefits. Upon completion of the fruits, we shall immediately move to the vegetables, listing each vegetable and identifying its traits and health benefits and then to the seeds, nuts and grains.

Fruits

Apple

Apples supply a variety of vitamins and minerals, including Vitamins A, B_1, B_2, B_6, C and E, pantothenic acid, folic acid, biotin, chromium, calcium, iron, magnesium, manganese, phosphorus, potassium, silicon and sulfur. Apples strengthen the blood and aid in maintaining a healthy liver and kidneys as well as healthy respiratory and digestive systems. When eaten whole, they are good for keeping the teeth clean and stimulating the gums. Apples act as a cleanser, as do all fruits and are thus helpful for cleansing the intestinal tract, removing toxins from the body generally and maintaining healthy, clear skin. I have found apple juice to have a tremendous soothing effect on the body, settling tension, stress and nervous conditions. An apple a day really does keep the doctor away. When buying apples, make sure that they are very firm, unbruised and fully colored. Make every attempt possible to buy whole, organic apples, and if you're not sure of their being organic, make sure you avoid those that are coated with a wax. This wax is a true sign that they have been chemicalized.

Apricot

Apricots are good sources of vitamin A, iron and manganese with substantial amounts of the B vitamins, vitamin C, calcium, magnesium, phosphorous, potassium and sulfur. Apricots are good for treating anemia and cleansing the blood and respiratory system. I have used combinations of apricot juice and cayenne pepper very successfully for cleansing impurities from the blood and besides, apricot juice is delicious! Apricots have also been noted as being good for treating lung cancer. When selecting apricots, make sure they are a sunripened yellow-orange, not mushy or bruised. It is best to buy organic, unsprayed apricots, because you definitely want to eat the skin!

Avocado

Avocados are very high in vitamins B_1 and B_6 and potassium. They also contain vitamins A, B_2, B_3 and C, calcium, copper, iron, magnesium and phosphorus. Avocados are soothing for those with ulcers and for those with inflamed conditions of the mucous membranes, small intestines and colon. They are also good for impotence, constipation, insomnia and nervousness. I actually consider avocado to be a superfood. It is a fruit that when eaten well can definitely build the body muscle. Although I am not concerned with a big muscular frame, I have used avocados combined with green leafy vegetables in directing others to amass that "powerful look." While living in Africa and Asia, my family and I used avocado as a basic staple food, especially when combined well with some nice habanera peppers, some fresh cayenne and (sweet) potato leaves or spinach. Or in a fruit combination with bananas, it is wonderful. Besides, for a man with large spiritual matehood responsibilities, avocado is one of the major foods that will serve him well. Please be very careful when picking avocados. Make sure that the skin texture is smoothed and tight and not wrinkled in any manner at all. If the skin is loose, the avocado may be overripe/rancid. Please feel the large end of the avocado which should give to gentle pressure. If it is too hard, this means that the avocado was picked too soon, and the fruit may rot before it ripens.

Banana

Bananas are best noted for being high in potassium. They also contain substantial amounts of vitamin A, the B vitamins, especially B_6, biotin, calcium, magnesium, manganese, phosphorus, sulfur, chlorine and sodium. After reviewing the vitamin and mineral content of bananas, I'm sure you can see why I identify bananas as a super food. If you could have the experience of having a banana plantation and witnessing their process from birth to maturity, you would definitely walk away with a new consciousness about food birth, and you would definitely want to eat more bananas. Bananas have a soothing effect on the digestive system and are very calming to the central nervous system. They are also an excellent energy food. I have used the skins to treat skin burns and ulcerated and infected skin conditions. It should be well noted that bananas are one of those foods that serve womanhood well, while also being of tremendous assistance in increasing the energy level of the man. Bananas supply energy to the woman during her menstrual cycle and help to soothe menstrual cramps and aches. I utilized a live holistic diet with lots of bananas with one of the spiritual mates of the Royal Family who had suffered from severe menstrual cramps for a period of eighteen years. Within a matter of weeks, she was pain free and able to throw out hundreds of dollars worth of herbal and vitamin supplements. She is still singing the praises of bananas to this day. We use bananas as the first whole foods for the children after leaving the breast milk of the mother. We also find bananas very useful in preparing our live cakes, pies and puddings. They are the natural and divine alternative to the dead and devitalized commodities used when baking the dead and devitalized versions of these items. Bananas are best eaten when they are spotted. This is when they are the sweetest. When they go past that stage, they can serve in the same capacity to sweeten as medjool or honey ball dates. Bananas are also a staple food of our family and should be considered as a staple food of any live foodist.

Blackberries

Blackberries are highest in calcium, Vitamin C and iron. They also contain significant amounts of Vitamins A and B complex, magnesium, potassium, phosphorus and sulfur. Blackberries are good blood and intestinal cleansers. I have used blackberries in juice and puree form to treat sore joints and also to provide a very tasty meal. As are all live foods, blackberries are an excellent food that also serves as an herb. When buying blackberries and all berries, make sure that they are firm and are in full color from head to toe. Be very watchful of mold. Blackberries, as with all berries and grapes, should be as organic as possible, plus. Sprays and chemical treatments should be avoided at all costs.

Blueberries

Blueberries contain significant amounts of Vitamin C, iron, calcium, B_6 and the B-complex vitamins, phosphorus and vitamin A. Blueberries are good blood cleansers and have good antiseptic properties. They aid in proper elimination and keeping the skin clear. Blueberries are one of the fruits that I have often recommended for people with ulcerated conditions. I've also used blueberries in wounds when other items were not available. They are excellent in getting rid of germs, and they are very tasty. You would love our live, life blueberry pie. I'm telling you that it tastes so good, it will make you cry.

Breadfruit

Breadfruit is high in calcium and contains significant quantities of vitamins A, B_1, B_2, B_3, C, iron and phosphorus. Breadfruit is an excellent body builder. When unripe, breadfruit is starchy. However, when allowed to ripen, this fruit is non-starchy and sweet. It is very filling and especially recommended in cases of underweight.

Carob

Carob contains vitamins A and B complex, calcium, phosphorus, iron and copper. It is good for healthy teeth and bones and building the red blood. Carob is also good for diarrhea. First of all, it is very difficult to find raw carob for some reason. For commercial purposes, they seem to want to roast and toast all of the life and excellent taste out of it. We use carob in our live, life pies, our sunchild's carob cake and in so many of our carob drinks. If you are not fortunate enough to find raw carob powder, our suggestion is to buy raw carob beans and grind them into a powder. From there your creativity will take you into a world of live life carob/chocolate capable of mixing and blending with other fruits such as dates to make something wonderful. You can make yourself a delicious carob-covered apple, especially tasty with ground nuts sprinkled over it. And I have to tell you that one of my favorite combinations is carob banana with live almond nut butter.

Cherries

Cherries and cherry juice are highest in vitamins A and C. They also contain significant amounts of calcium, magnesium, phosphorus, potassium, iron and silicon, as well as vitamins B_1, B_2, E, folic acid and niacin. Cherries are good blood, liver, kidney and intestinal cleansers. They also aid in healing respiratory ailments as well as in conditions involving inflammation of the joints. Please see blackberries for selection information. Yes, we do make a live, life cherry pie.

Coconut

Coconuts are fruits and seeds in and of themselves. They are extra special whole foods. Coconuts contain healthy quantities of vitamins B_1 (thiamine), B_2, B_3 and C, calcium, iodine, magnesium, potassium, phosphorus and iron. Coconut is an excellent intestinal cleanser and body builder. It is good for digestive ailments, including stomach ulcers and constipation. Coconuts alone are capable of wholly nourishing the body. I can recall a time during the war era in West Africa when my family and I lived totally on coconuts, and I can recall other times when we lived solely on sweet and soursaps. These are two fruits that provide all the water or juice content that you need. Coconuts, as do palm nuts, have the capacity to maintain, build and supply all of the food nourishment needed by the body. Not only is coconut a very wholesome food, it has many other practical uses for body care, maintenance and even for body protection—inside and out.

For example, we use the oil to heal cuts, scratches and burns and as a hair and skin oil. Coconut oil can be made right at home by juicing the hard coconut into a milk and letting it sit. Make sure that you drink as much of the milk as possible, because it is an excellent food. In some cases, we have used the coconut milk to feed a child whose mother was unable to breast feed. Remember, when the coconut milk sits for a while, the cream rises to the top, and the oil sits above the cream. We have found coconut oil, coconut cream and coconut milk to be excellent in inspiring hair growth. It best serves you when you take it both internally and externally. As I've said, coconuts are *the* superfood—one of the few items on this planet that you could eat and receive the bulk of whole living nourishment.

Cranberries

Cranberries and cranberry juice are highest in vitamins A, B complex, C, folic acid and sulfur and contain significant quantities of calcium, iodine, iron, phosphorus and potassium. Cranberries are good for cleansing the kidney and liver. As cleansers, they help to keep the skin clear and healthy. They aid in relieving lung congestion, and the juice is noted for treating urinary tract disorders. When selecting cranberries, try to select the darkest berries. The darker the berry, the sweeter the juice. Yes, it is possible to make living live cranberry sauce. All you need is a good mortar and pestle. A mortar and pestle is a blender-like mechanism carved out of wood and used throughout Afrika. You take ripened cranberries and put them in the mortar, then take the pestle and pound them until they are soft. When ripe, cranberries have a nice sweet taste. However, there are some other natural fruits that can be added as sweeteners. Cranberries also make a super-nutritious juice that is actually an herbal tonic for the liver, lungs and urinary tract.

Cucumber

Cucumber is high in sodium, sulfur, iodine, silicon, potassium, phosphorus and chlorine. It also contains vitamins A, B_1, B_2 and C, calcium and iron. Cucumber is an excellent diuretic, encouraging urination. We've found it to be excellent for stimulating hair growth. I have used it to treat sore joints and high and low blood pressure. Cucumber also helps to maintain healthy teeth, gums, nails and skin. For those who don't know, we have a lot of long hair in our family, even at my young age of over a half a century plus. One of the primary reasons is our vital consumption of cucumbers. While in West Africa, it was a common occurrence for our dining table to be filled with cucumber soups, cucumber juice and cucumber salads. Especially during the times of war and conflict in the specific area where we were located, we would take the seeds, dry them, plant some and eat some and prepare for the massive growth of cucumbers that came from them. Cucumbers and cayenne pepper serves as a super tonic for the body. Since we had cucumbers in such abundance, we would use the juice to wash our hair. Now, that is super, refreshing and gives a superb feeling to the scalp. When selecting cucumbers, make sure the skin is firm and not soft or wrinkled. Avoid cucumbers that have any mushy spots at all. Whatever you do, do not buy waxed cucumbers. If you do, peel the skins. If you can buy organic, do; and eat everything, skin, seeds and all.

Dates

Dates are high in vitamin B_3 (niacin), calcium, potassium, chlorine and iron. They also contain significant amounts of vitamins A, B_1 and B_2, magnesium and phosphorus. Dates are easily digested, very high in carbohydrates and thus good for energy. Dates are good for treating anemia, low blood pressure, stomach ulcers, hemorrhoids, colitis, gum disease, tuberculosis, sexual impotency and nervous conditions. They can be made into a syrup for coughs, sore throat and bronchitis. Let it be known that dates are right on the verge of being a superfood according to our definition. No, in fact, they are a superfood. Although very sweet in texture, we have used dates consistently over the past 30 years to stimulate the milk flow from the mother's breast. In my prior years as an athlete, I used dates for that extra burst of energy that made me a winner in both basketball and bowling.

Dates are definitely a divine food of the sun, and it is absolutely amazing that they come right off the tree as a soft, tender, honey-sweet fruit. Dates are excellent with nuts. Just remove the pit and replace it with a nice brazil nut, or pecan, or if you like, let the almond be the host of this occasion. We've long been noted for the fact that we use dates instead of honey to sweeten our live life pies, our living live cakes and our live puddings and energy smoothies. What I suggest is that you find your way to a location where you can buy yourself some jumbo medjool dates and treat yourself to the energy powerhouse of life. We prefer medjool and honey ball dates, as very high quality, very nutritious and very tasty. However, there are others with thicker skins, that are equally as nutritious. Never buy pitted dates. It is my firm belief that once the seed is removed from any fruit, the whole nutritional value of the fruit begins to alter. My studies show that the seed continues to provide a life source to the fruit in its divine evolution.

Eggplant

Eggplant is high in potassium and contains vitamins A, B_1, B_2, B_3 and C, iron, phosphorus and calcium. It is recommended in cases of constipation, colitis, stomach ulcers and for nerve conditions.

Figs

Figs are high in calcium and selenium. They also contain significant quantities of vitamins A, B_1, B_2, B_3 and C, iron, silicon and phosphorus. They are good for constipation, low blood pressure, anemia, colitis, under weight, asthma, tuberculosis, excess mucous production, inflammation of the joints and skin diseases. Within the Royal Family, there is a sisterhood member who suffered from Raynaud's disease, a condition where one has an extreme sensitivity to cold, losing circulation in the hands and feet, particularly the toes and fingers. The extremities turn blue or white from lack of blood flow, and it is very painful. A live foods diet, generally and figs in particular, has been found helpful in treating this condition, and up until present there is no sign that she still suffers from this ailment. Fig juice is a good laxative and good for sore throats, coughs and digestive ulcers. Figs can be used as a poultice for boils, skin and gum/teeth abscesses. If you have the opportunity to buy and consume fresh figs, please give your body that wonderful treat. We have fig trees growing in our gardens right now, but between the women and the children, I only get that treat every once in a while. It's amazing that a fruit that is so nutritious and wholesome is not more widely planted and distributed in its fresh form.

Grapes

Grapes are good sources of chromium and iodine. They also contain significant quantities of vitamins A, B_1, B_2, B_3, C, niacin, calcium, iron, magnesium, manganese, phosphorus, potassium, silicon and sulfur. Grapes are excellent body cleansers, cleansing and building the blood and cleansing the liver. Grapes are good for energy and stimulate the metabolism. Needless to say, grapes are one of those fruits that could easily be declared as a super food. As a matter of fact, in earlier times of ancient Kemet, grapes were considered the holy foods of the gods and goddesses and their most sacred representatives. The reputation continued until some of the offspring carried some of these juices to distant lands, where the length of travel fermented them into wines. I don't know whose foods they became then, when people began to get intoxicated off of them. But, until this day grapes are highly-touted as good for the blood. Let me make it clear that we're talking about whole, live, fresh, organic grapes and not its mutation, wine. If you really want a special treat, find yourself some organic champagne grapes and juice them up. Grape juice enters the blood quickly, and you can immediately feel its blood-cleansing and invigorating effect from head to toe, especially in the head. I guarantee you that whole, fresh, live, organic grapes will not intoxicate you while getting you high. When selecting grapes, buy organic grapes. Make sure they are firm and check the entire bunch; because one bad one can spoil the others. Smell them for freshness and avoid any sour-smelling bunch all together. Never buy grapes that are hard; they are not ripe. Be smart. Before buying, pick one from the bottom of the bunch and one from the stem, to test their sweetness.

Grapefruit

All citrus fruits are high in vitamin C and are also good sources of inositol. Grapefruits contain significant quantities of biotin and the other B vitamins, calcium, iron and phosphorus. Grapefruits aid in removing inorganic calcium that has formed in the cartilage of the joints. They are also natural antiseptics when used externally. I have also found them helpful in helping to burn away fatty tissue. Therefore, grapefruits are an excellent food for obese persons who wish to rid themselves of toxic fatty tissue.   As said consistently, when selecting grapefruits, make sure that they are fully colored. Not green. Make sure that they are firm all around, without soft spots. Soft spots on citrus is a sign of decay. As with all fruits, especially citrus, keep your nose open for mold-like smells. This is a sign that the fungus of decay is on the skin of the grapefruit, within it, or that there is a rotten grapefruit among the bunch.

Guavas

Guavas are excellent sources of vitamin C. They are also good sources of the B complex vitamins, especially niacin (B_1). Guavas contain significant quantities of vitamin A, calcium, iron and phosphorus. They are helpful in treating cases of diarrhea, high blood pressure, prolonged menstruation, poor circulation, asthma and acidosis—a condition that results from eating cooked, processed, dead and devitalized foods. Thus, I have used guavas with those who are transitioning to a live foods diet to balance their system. I should also note that there are stories about guava seeds being the cause of gallstones. On our large West African resort, guava was a daily part of our diet as long as it was in season, especially for those who were transitioning from a dead foods diet. We never had any sign of such a thing as gallstones. So please make sure you eat your seeds and chew them well for optimal nourishment. Guavas come in several varieties. There is a small golden-yellow one which has a pinkish flesh. There is a larger, more commercial variety which is greenish-gold with a milky flesh. These are the varieties that we are most familiar with and have found in the Caribbean, Central and South America, Africa and Asia. However, be sure that there are other varieties of this fruit. Guavas are sweet and pear-like in taste, though more tender in taste and flavor.

Lemons and Limes

Lemons and limes are a tremendous source of vitamin C. They also contain significant quantities of vitamins B_1 and B_3, calcium, phosphorus, potassium and iron. Lemons and limes are best known for their antiseptic properties and can be used internally and externally for this purpose. From our experience, lime is one of the best antiseptics in the world, followed closely by its cousin, the lemon. We use lime juice as a facial cleanser and a natural hair shampoo and conditioner. It can also be used to clean the teeth or, diluted with water, as a douche.

We use sliced lime or lemon and their juices, applying them directly to cuts, acne sores, boils and other skin sores. We have applied lime to insect bites, especially mosquito bites and other irritations for cleansing or relieving itching. While my family and I were living in West Africa, those in the neighboring villages often wondered why myself and my family never came down with malaria. I'm sure that a contributing factor is the fact that as soon as one of us would get a mosquito bite, we would scrub the bite with lime. Lemon and lime juice can also be used to relieve cold symptoms, such as cough and running nose. Before meals the juice can be taken, or it can be mixed with foods, in order to aid digestion. Lime and lemon are also effective in treating the following conditions: rheumatism, arthritis, liver ailments, asthma, colds, fever, pneumonia and neuritis. So, lime is definitely a superfoods antiseptic. In and of itself, it can become your total body care unit—from washing to treating scars and wounds.

Mango

Mangos are high in Vitamins A and C. They also contain significant amounts of Vitamins B_1, B_2 and B_3, calcium, iron and phosphorus. Mangos are beneficial for kidney conditions and are also good for digestive and respiratory ailments. Mango skins can be applied externally to clogged pores and cysts, but be careful, because flies love them. It is best to eat the entire mango, skin and all. Probably the reason there are so many mangos in the tropics is that the mango seed is very difficult to consume. There are too many varieties of mangos to list them all here. We had more than twelve different varieties growing on our resort in West Africa. When selecting mangos, make sure that they are very firm and golden yellow or golden orange. Avoid selecting mangos that are green and hard. They may have been picked to soon and may turn green and soft on you. Be especially wary of mangos that are green and soft; these have little flavor. You can tell a fresh picked mango by the stem and the milky and glue-like substance that comes from it.

Melon (watermelon, casaba melon, cantaloupe, musk melon, honeydew)

Cantaloupe, in particular, is very high in vitamin A and a good source of folic acid and vitamins B5 and B_6. All melons have significant amounts of vitamin C, the B complex vitamins, calcium, iron, magnesium, sulfur, phosphorus and potassium. Watermelons are particularly rich in potassium. Melons are natural diuretics and are helpful in relieving kidney and bladder conditions. Melons are also recommended in cases of rheumatism, arthritis, high blood pressure, gas, skin diseases and blood deficiencies. I've often encouraged persons who suffer from anemia to consume lots of watermelon, especially the seeds. It has been reported and I have found, that watermelon juice with the seeds is helpful in reducing high blood pressure. For selection, please review the shopping section above.

Okra

Okra is high in calcium, sodium and potassium and contains vitamins A, B_3 (niacin) and C and small traces of B_1, B_2, iron, sulfur and phosphorus. Okra is good for treating stomach ulcers and inflammation of the lungs (pleurisy) and the colon (colitis). Okra has been recommended in cases of sore throat and obesity.

Olives

Olives have significant quantities of vitamin A, calcium, iron and phosphorus. Olive oil stimulates contractions of the gall bladder, is a good nerve tonic and will help to strengthen and develop the body tissue. Olives are good for liver disorders, diabetes, abdominal gas, indigestion and constipation. The oil is good for burns, sunburn and minor skin eruptions and inflammations. Olive oil is also good for soothing ear infections and for the removal of earwax. Olive oil makes an excellent hair tonic, stimulating hair growth as well as aiding in preventing hair loss. Needless to say olives, especially extra virgin olive oil, would have to be declared as a superfood. Extra virgin olive oil has a reputation that goes back to the earliest dynasties of the Divine Children of the Sun. Extra virgin olive oil is the only oil used in our household other than those that we make ourselves from fresh nuts and seeds in a manner that does not include the application of heat. If you happen to be someone who has a love for olives, we suggest that you be very careful in your selection process. Seek out a Mediterranean store that sells the olives whole. Identify the olives that are pre-soaked in olive oil and sun evaporated sea water. After purchasing these olives, it is our advice that you carry them home very gently without tasting, get yourself of a bottle of cold-pressed apple cider vinegar, wash them very thoroughly and pre-soak them in the vinegar for a couple of days. After they have soaked in the vinegar, soak them an additional day in some extra virgin olive oil before consuming. Once they have gone through this process, they can be stored in extra virgin olive oil for at least one day. Now, prepare for a delicious treat. What is especially delicious is to store the olives in an olive oil, lime, garlic and pepper dressing for at least three days (after soaking them in vinegar) for extra flavor. When you open them and fix them inside of your green, leafy salad, the only thing that I can say is "Wow! What a treat!"

Orange

Oranges are high in vitamins C and A and also contain significant quantities of iodine, vitamins B_1, B_2, B_6, K, biotin, folic acid, inositol and niacin, calcium, iron, magnesium, phosphorus, potassium and zinc. Oranges are good for clearing the respiratory and gastrointestinal tracts, keeping them healthy and in aiding in conditions involving inflammation of the joints. For those who are changing their diets from a dead and devitalized diet to a live foods diet, oranges seem to have been designed with you in mind. Drinking orange juice helps with food cravings and cravings for alcohol. I've also utilized orange juice to assist in cutting down on the craving for nicotine with smokers.

Pawpaw (Papaya)

Papayas are very high in Vitamins A, C, D, E and K. They also contain significant amounts of calcium, iron, phosphorus, potassium and silicon. Papayas contain the digestive enzyme, papain, which aids in digestion. Papayas are a natural cleanser and tonic for the digestive system and intestinal tract and help to cleanse the kidneys and liver. Papayas also aid in clotting the blood. I have used the pulp and the skin and the juicy milk-like substance to heal lacerations, cuts and bruises. When picking pawpaw, please make sure that you do not pick them too green.

Always shake them to feel the weight of the seeds. Light-weighted seeds are a sign of immaturity. The yellower the pawpaw, the better.

Peach

The peach and its juice are high in vitamin A. Peaches also contain significant quantities of iron, phosphorus, potassium, calcium, magnesium and vitamins B_1, B_2, B_3 and C. Peaches are recommended to treat anemia, constipation, high blood pressure, inflammation of the stomach, inflammation of the kidneys, inflammation of the bronchial tubes, asthma and kidney and bladder stones. They are good for skin health. Peaches are intestinal cleansers used in removing worms. They are very soothing to the digestive system and are good for women who are suffering from morning sickness. When selecting peaches, please make sure that you do not select this fruit green or hard, because these have a tendency to mold and rot before they ripen. Peaches are exceptional in taste when they are tender. Avoid peaches that are mushy or that are bruised.

Pears

Pears contain significant amounts of Vitamins A, B_1, B_2, B_3 and C, folic acid, phosphorus, potassium, calcium, iron, magnesium and sulfur. Pears are good for digestion, as are all fruits, relieving constipation and inflammation of the kidneys and colon. Pears are also diuretics. See apples for selection criteria.

Peppers (Bell)

Peppers are fruits. They are a good source of vitamin C, potassium and silicon. Peppers also contain significant quantities of vitamins A, B_1, B_2 and B_3, calcium, iron, phosphorus and potassium. Red pepper is especially high in vitamin A. Peppers are good for clearing skin blemishes. They are also recommended for liver disorders, obesity, constipation, gas, high blood pressure, improving circulation, toning and cleansing the arteries and heart muscle and acidosis. Peppers are also good for the hair, nails and skin.

Peppers (Hot)

Hot peppers are higher in sulfur, calcium, phosphorus, vitamins A, B complex and C than sweet peppers. First and foremost, hot peppers like cayenne are superb blood cleansers. Cayenne and other hot peppers are very helpful with infections like malaria and other diseases of the blood. Hot peppers are also recommended for colds, asthma, inflamed sinuses and the removal of intestinal worms. Hot peppers open your taste buds, giving you the opportunity to really enjoy and appreciate the live flavors of the foods with which they are combined. An approach that we have within the royal household is to eat a peppered dish before consuming some of our favorite dishes. This approach is exceptional in bringing out the flavor in any whole and live vegetable, seed, nut, or grain dish.

Persimmon

Persimmons contain significant amounts of vitamins A, B_1, B_2 and C, iron, phosphorus and potassium. They are very soothing to the intestinal tract and are therefore helpful in treating intestinal ulcers, constipation, colitis and hemorrhoids. Persimmons have also been used to treat inflammation of the membrane that covers the lung (pleurisy). They are also very soothing to the throat as well as soothing and tantalizing to the tongue, especially in an exotic live life persimmon pie. When selecting persimmons, be very careful not to select fruit with hard spots at the base or head. They should be very smooth and firm, but not hard in texture. When the fruit ripens, it has a tendency to burst easily. Persimmons must be eaten immediately upon ripening, when they are most sweet. If eaten before they are ripe, persimmons leave a very untasty ash on your tongue. Look for the beautiful dark orange texture and you will know that you have selected a delicious fruit.

Pineapple

Pineapples are high in Vitamins B_1 and C, manganese, chlorine and potassium. They also contain vitamins A, B_2 and B_3, calcium, iodine, iron, magnesium and phosphorus. Pineapples contain the enzyme bromelain, a live enzyme which acts as an anti-inflammatory. Pineapple is helpful for constipation, enlargement of the thyroid gland (goiter), inflammation of the bronchial tubes (bronchitis), arthritis, high blood pressure, removing intestinal worms and treating sore throat and other throat infections. Coconut milk has a lot of protein in it and what I have found is that the digestive enzymes in pineapple cause it to combine exceptionally well with the milk of this wonder fruit. When peeling pineapple, one should be very careful of the skin and to avoid the seeds in the skin. These are so powerful that they can burn and irritate the tongue and mouth. There are some pineapples that ripen when they are partially green and there are some that ripen when they are a bright orange yellow. The key is to be familiar with the species of pineapple that you are selecting and to be aware that green pineapples will definitely irritate the system.

Plantain

Plantains contain significant amounts of vitamins A, B_1, B_2, B_3 and C, calcium, iron and phosphorus. They are high in carbohydrates and a good source of energy. Plantain is an excellent "big banana." Most people have never eaten a ripe plantain. In fact there are very few ripe plantains that have been eaten by the populations that deal with them. We prepare several superb live plantain dishes. Plantains are excellent when ripened and combined with cayenne pepper and selected spices. When selecting plantains for purchase, please keep in mind that it is a whole live life food with a tremendous amount of live life enzymes. Any degree or form of murder of the plantain, be it baking, boiling, or frying will kill its live life enzymes. Although it has become a tradition among folks to fry, boil, or bake them, for the best possible taste and the highest nutrition, the best possible way of preparing them is fresh, raw and live. When selecting plantains, ripeness is determined by how soft the fruit is. Avoid selecting hard, green, or unripe plantains. The more black within the yellow skin, the better.

Plum

Plums contain Vitamins A, B_1, B_2, B_3 and C, iron, potassium, calcium, magnesium and phosphorus. Plums aid in digestion and elimination. They are also helpful for liver disorders, bronchitis and skin eruptions. When buying plums, look for firm yet soft skin and darkness of color. Always remember that sweet plums are very sour when they are hard.

Pomegranate

The pomegranate contains Vitamins B_1, B_2 and B_3, iron and potassium and small amounts of Vitamin C, calcium and phosphorus. Pomegranates are excellent body cleansers, having a cleansing effect on the blood and liver. Pomegranates are not only delicious just to eat, but they also make an excellent juice, seeds and all. Strangely enough, the pomegranate used to be known as the Indian apple, which is a clear indication that the Native American Children of the Sun prized them for consumption. For sweetness, pomegranates should be purchased when as deep a red as possible. They should be firm, yet gentle to the touch. Avoid purchasing a mushy pomegranate or one that has begun to turn purple instead of a deep, dark red. This pomegranate has begun to rot.

Prunes

Prunes are sundried plums. Prunes are high in vitamins A and B_3 (niacin), magnesium, iron, potassium and phosphorus. They also have significant amounts of vitamins B_1, B_2 and C and calcium. Prunes are good for blood circulation, anemia, constipation and hemorrhoids. Prune juice is a good remedy for sore throat. As we said, prunes are sundried plums. I think we have to create another name for a plum that has been dehydrated. All that is to say, you should make sure that your prunes are sundried, unsulfured and without additives, preservatives, artificial flavors, or colors.

Raisins

Raisins are sundried grapes. Raisins are high in calcium, chromium, copper, magnesium, iron, phosphorus and potassium. They also contain significant quantities of biotin, vitamins A, B_1, B_2, B_3 and B_6. They are a good energy food, used in cases of underweight and anemia. They have been used in cases of tuberculosis, low blood pressure, constipation and heart disease. I have often utilized and recommended the utilization of raisins soaked in fresh-squeezed apple juice as a syrup to treat sore throat, asthma and excess mucous production. It is very necessary that the juice used for soaking is freshly squeezed so as to maintain all of the life enzymes in the fruit and juice. The proportion of juice used should be small, just enough for the fruits to soak it up, so that it can be squeezed back out as a syrup. You will know when the raisins have soaked long enough, because they will swell up and begin to look like grapes again. As with prunes, make sure that your raisins are sundried, unsulfured and additive- and preservative-free.

Raspberries

Raspberries are high in magnesium, iron and biotin, containing significant amounts of vitamins B_1, B_2, B_3 and C. They also contain calcium, iron, phosphorus and potassium. Raspberries are good intestinal and liver cleansers. They aid with menstrual cramps and high blood pressure.

Soursap/Sweetsap

Soursap is one of the most nutritious foods, supplying virtually every known vitamin and mineral and has been used for treating obesity. It is one of those foods that could be declared whole enough to sustain one's life in and of itself. Soursap is a juicy fruit. While living in West Africa, I have lived on soursap alone for extensive periods of time without losing an ounce of weight or an ounce of energy. Soursaps resemble a fat yam, except they grow on trees. The skin is a light greenish-tan or a light tannish-brown on the outside and a creamy color on the inside with an abundance of black seeds. Soursaps should be eaten just ripe. When overripe, the taste is too dull to eat and when under-ripe the fruit is too hard and dull-tasting to eat. When ripe, the soursap is firm and gives gently to the touch. Be aware that when the skin begins to look burnt and shiny, the fruit has started to rot. Soursap juice is actually a whole nourishment tonic in and of itself; however, you may need a press or an organized mortar and pestle system to properly extract the juice. When it comes to nutritionally valued foods, coconuts and soursaps stand out in a class of their own. Add a few dark green leafy vegetables, and you are set. Actually with just these two fruits, you can survive without the dark green leafies for quite some time if you have to.

Strawberries

Strawberries are good sources of vitamin C, calcium, phosphorus, selenium, sodium and potassium. They also contain vitamins A, B_1, B_2, B_3 and E, iron and magnesium. Strawberries are good cleansers for the blood, liver and skin. They have been used to treat gout, rheumatism, high blood pressure, skin cancer and syphilis. Strawberries can be put directly on sore eyes or on the skin to treat ringworm. Strawberries can also be used to clean tartar from teeth and to strengthen the gums.

Tomato

Tomatoes are high in vitamins A and C, biotin, sodium, calcium, potassium, silicon, magnesium and chlorine. Tomatoes also contain inositol, vitamins B_1, B_2, B_3 and K, phosphorus and iron. The tomato is a liver cleanser and stimulates circulation and the heart. It is a natural antiseptic and blood cleanser and purifier, protecting against infection. Tomatoes improve the skin, because they are such good cleansers of toxic waste in the blood. I have used tomatoes or recommended their usage in treating cases of gout, rheumatism, tuberculosis, high blood pressure, high cholesterol, sinus trouble, liver congestion, gallstones, gas, colds, high cholesterol and obesity. I have received many testimonials of their effectiveness in treating these conditions. I have used the skins, by applying them externally, to treat ringworm, pus-filled sores and acne. The Vitamin K in tomatoes helps to prevent hemorrhages, by aiding in blood clotting. I'm sure that you can see that tomatoes are definitely a wonder food. Tomatoes serve as an internal and external first aid kit and fruit for our household. Someone should have coined the phrase: A tomato a day keeps the doctor away.

Note: As with all foods, tomatoes are very detrimental to the system if eaten cooked, especially when combined with concentrated starches, *e.g.* combinations like pizza, pasta with tomato sauce, etc. When cooked, tomatoes become acidic, leaching minerals from tissues, teeth and bones.

Vegetables

Alfalfa Sprouts

Alfalfa sprouts are high in vitamins A, B complex, C, E and K and calcium, chlorine, magnesium, iodine, phosphorus, potassium, selenium, silicon, sodium and zinc. Alfalfa sprouts are a good overall tonic due to their high vitamin and mineral content.

Asparagus

Asparagus is high in vitamins A, B_1 (thiamine), C, E, choline, folic acid, PABA, manganese, potassium, silicon, sulfur and iron. It aids in breaking up oxalic acid crystals in the kidneys and muscles and is thus helpful for conditions such as rheumatism, neuritis and arthritis. Let's make it very clear that asparagus is one of the most exciting live foods delicacies to prepare and consume. It can be shredded or finely sliced and prepared so deliciously.

Beets

Beets are high in vitamins A and C, calcium, iron, potassium and sodium. They also contain significant amounts of folic acid, vitamin B_6, choline, chromium, fluorine, magnesium, manganese, potassium, phosphorus, silicon and sulfur. Beets are excellent blood-builders, building the red corpuscles. The beet is also a powerful blood and liver cleanser. It is helpful for menstrual difficulties and menopause. Beets are good for treating headaches, toothaches, inflammation of kidneys and bladder and kidney stones, leukemia, tumors, constipation, liver ailments, inflammation of the intestines, anemia, lumbago and nervousness.

Beet Greens (and other green leafy vegetables: collard greens, dandelion greens, turnip greens, mustard greens, kale and spinach)

All green leafy vegetables are potent body healers in that they rebuild the cell structure of the body. All leafy green vegetables are high in vitamins A, B_1, B_2, B_3, B5, B_6, C, E and K, folic acid, choline, fluorine, inositol, PABA, calcium, chlorine, chromium, copper, iodine, iron, silicon, magnesium and manganese. Beet greens also contain sodium. They are helpful in treating anemia, constipation, poor appetite, inflammation of mucous membranes of the intestine (dysentery), skin disorders, gas, gout, tumors, tonsillitis, obesity, tuberculosis and gonorrhea.

(**Note:** Greens such as beet greens, turnip greens, mustard greens, kale, collard greens and spinach have very high amounts of organic oxalic acid which is very good for the body as it aids in digestion and combines readily with calcium, aiding in its digestion and assimilation. Cooking renders the oxalic acid in these vegetables inorganic and toxic, combining with the calcium in the food and rendering it unusable).

Broccoli

Broccoli is high in Vitamins A, B_1, B_2, B_3, B5, C and K, folic acid, PABA, calcium and sulfur. It also contains vitamin E, iron, magnesium, manganese, selenium and potassium. Broccoli aids in digestion and elimination.

Cabbage

Cabbage is high in vitamins B5, B_6, C, K, chlorine, iodine, silicon, sulfur and potassium. It also contains selenium and vitamin E. Cabbage is an excellent cleanser, particularly for the mucous membranes of the stomach and intestines. It is also a good blood cleanser and aids in maintaining healthy teeth, gums, hair, nails and bones. Cabbage is also helpful treating kidney and bladder disorders. My recommendation that cabbage juice be used for treating ulcers has been proven very successful over the years, especially when combined with a whole, live diet.

Carrots

Carrots are excellent sources of vitamin A, iodine, potassium and sodium. They also contain vitamins B_1, B_2, B_3, B5, C, D, E and K, folic acid, calcium, chlorine, magnesium, manganese, iron, phosphorus, sodium, sulfur and silicon. Carrots aid in digestion and help to maintain healthy hair, nails, skin and eyesight. The juice aids in preventing infection of the eyes, throat, tonsils, sinuses and respiratory organs. The carrot is an excellent liver and intestinal cleanser. It also protects the nervous system. Carrots are recommended for treating ulcerous and cancerous conditions. Carrot juice should be consumed daily by every live foodist and it is especially suitable for pregnant and nursing mothers. I've often recommended carrot juice for individuals suffering from stress, tension and other common mental disorders.

Cauliflower

Cauliflower is high in vitamins B_5, C and K, iron and sulfur. It also contains vitamins A, B_1, B_2 and B_3, calcium, phosphorus, copper, fluorine and magnesium. Cauliflower is a good blood purifier. It is recommended in cases of kidney and bladder disorders, obesity, high blood pressure, gout, improper secretion and flow of bile and constipation.

Celery

Celery is high in calcium, sodium, magnesium, manganese, chlorine, iron and iodine. It also contains vitamins B_1, B_2, B_3 and C, chlorine, silicon, phosphorus and potassium. It has a calming effect on the nervous system and is good for the blood, lungs and bronchial system. Celery has been recommended in treating diseases of the kidney, arthritis, rheumatism, neuritis, constipation, asthma, high blood pressure, excess mucous production, inflammation of the gums and loosening of teeth (pyorrhea), diabetes, brain fatigue, acidosis, gallstones, obesity, tuberculosis, anemia and insomnia. Because of its iodine content, celery serves as an excellent seasoning with other vegetables, nuts, seeds and grains.

Collard Greens

All green leafy vegetables are potent body healers in that they rebuild the cell structure of the body. All leafy green vegetables are high in vitamins A, B_1, B_2, B_3, B_5, B_6, C, E and K, folic acid, choline, fluorine, inositol, PABA, calcium, chlorine, chromium, copper, iodine, iron, magnesium and manganese. Collards are especially high in vitamins A, B_1, B_2 and B_3. Collards are good for anemia, liver trouble, acidosis, rheumatism, constipation, neuritis, arthritis, obesity and treating drug poisoning.

Corn

Corn is high in vitamin B_1, sulfur and magnesium. It also contains vitamins A, B_2, B_3, C and E, calcium, iron and phosphorus. It is recommended in cases of anemia, constipation and underweight. It must be remembered that fresh-picked/young corn is not a starchy food, but a sugar. The sugar in corn turns to starch, especially when it is not fresh picked, delayed in the storage process, or removed from the cob. It is therefore very important to consume corn as a fresh-picked commodity. Delayed consumption automatically feeds the body starch, a commodity that the body does not need, because it produces its own organic starch.

Dandelion Greens

All green leafy vegetables are potent body healers in that they rebuild the cell structure of the body. All leafy green vegetables are high in vitamins A, B_1, B_2, B_3, B_5, B_6, C, E and K, folic acid, choline, fluorine, inositol, PABA, calcium, chlorine, chromium, copper, iodine, iron, silicon, magnesium and manganese. In particular, dandelion greens are high in vitamins A and B_1, chromium, sodium, iron and potassium. They are also a good source of the magnesium and calcium needed to prevent bone and tooth loss and degeneration during pregnancy and to build the bones and teeth of the child. Dandelion greens are blood and cell builders, especially beneficial for the lungs and nervous system. They strengthen the bowels, muscle and skeletal system. Also, dandelion greens cleanse the blood, liver, gallbladder and spleen. They have been recommended in cases of anemia, low blood pressure, eczema, constipation, emaciation, cancerous tumors, syphilis and gonorrhea.

Dulse and Other Sea Vegetables

These super, dark green vegetables are extremely nourishing, because they are grown under water. When naturally and organically grown, they provide a source of nutrients that is not available in foods grown on top of the soil. All sea vegetables are excellent "brain" foods. Some other super sea vegetables are kelp, wakame, kombu, arame, hijiki, nori, sea moss and spirulina. They contain vitamins $B1_2$ and K, organic sodium, organic iron, magnesium, manganese and chlorine. All sea vegetables are detoxifiers and blood cleansers.

Dulse is a high-protein food and a super source of iron. Like all sea vegetables, it has a very high mineral content, containing high quantities of organic iodine, potassium, phosphorus and organic sodium. It is recommended to correct mineral deficiencies, anemia (due to its high iron content), for poor digestion, enlargement of the thyroid (because of its high iodine content) and for proper gland function. Dulse is said to be beneficial for impotence and under-weight.

Endive

Endive is a good source of Vitamin A, B_1 (thiamine), calcium, chlorine, potassium, sodium, phosphorus and iron. Endive is similar to dandelion greens. Endive is good for the optic nerve and muscle. It has been recommended in cases of asthma, hay fever, tuberculosis, for skin infections, gout, diabetes, constipation, rheumatism, anemia, high blood pressure, excess mucous production (catarrh), liver ailments, arthritis, neuritis, acidosis and gas.

Garlic

Garlic is high in selenium, B_1 (thiamine), sulfur and phosphorus. It also contains significant quantities of vitamins B_2, B_3 and C, iron and potassium. Onion and garlic are said to keep evil spirits away and I believe it is true. Because anytime I eat garlic, all of the people with a superficial, artificial and unnatural frame of thought tend to run away from me and they are definitely the evil spirits of the planet. Keeping the evil spirits away is notable enough; however, garlic has an extra potent ability to cleanse the blood and the body system, helping to eliminate toxins and waste from the body also making it good for the lymph. Garlic also aids in digestion and is recommended for treatment of colds, asthma, catarrh, bronchitis, fever, gas, hypothyroid condition, hardening of the arteries, sinusitis and promoting expectoration of phlegm and mucous.

Horseradish

Horseradish is high in calcium, sulfur and iron and contains vitamins B_1 (thiamine) and C and phosphorus. It acts as a solvent and cleanser, dissolving excess mucous in the system, especially in the nose and sinus areas. Therefore, it is recommended to treat colds, coughs and asthma. It also aids in digestion. Take equal amounts of fresh squeezed lime juice combined with horseradish juice for colds.

Kale

All green leafy vegetables are potent body healers in that they rebuild the cell structure of the body. All leafy green vegetables are high in vitamins A, B1, B_2, B_3, B_5, B_6, C, E and K, folic acid, choline, fluorine, inositol, PABA, calcium, chlorine, chromium, copper, iodine, iron, silicon, magnesium and manganese. Kale is especially high in vitamins A, B1 and B_3. It is good for constipation, obesity, acidosis, teeth, gums, arthritis, gout, rheumatism, skin disease and bladder disorders. (See cabbage for juicing benefits). We find kale to be excellent with spinach. Kale is also excellent when combined with carrot and parsley as a juice tonic for the eyes.

Kelp

Kelp is a good source of vitamins B_2 (riboflavin) and B_3 (niacin) and an excellent source of calcium, iron, iodine and phosphorus. It is a good source of minerals, generally and contains small amounts of Vitamin A. (See Dulse for health benefits).

Lettuce

Lettuce is high in vitamin E and iodine, iron and magnesium and is also a good source of vitamins A, B1, B_2, B_3, calcium, iron and potassium. It contains vitamin C, chlorine, manganese, sulfur, silicon and phosphorus. Romaine lettuce is especially high in vitamins and minerals and is rich in sodium. Its magnesium content makes it good for the muscles, brain, nerves and lungs. The silicon and sulfur content makes it good for the skin and hair, promoting hair growth. Its silicon content also makes it good for the muscles and joints. Lettuce is helpful for relaxing the nerves and is thus helpful in cases of insomnia and nervousness. It is a diuretic and is recommended for gastric disorders, anemia, constipation, catarrh, tuberculosis, circulatory disease, gout, poor appetite, urinary tract diseases, rheumatism and arthritis. Lettuce stimulates the adrenal gland and the production of adrenaline.

Mung Bean Sprouts/Soy bean sprouts

Mung bean and soy bean sprouts are very similar, but here we use mung bean sprouts as the example. Sprouts are high in folic acid, inositol, PABA and potassium. They also contain significant amounts of vitamins A, B1, B_2, B_3, B12, C, E and K, calcium, iron and phosphorus. Sprouts help to eliminate toxic poisons from the system. Sprouts are at their maximum absorbability in terms of the body's ability to assimilate them.

Mushrooms

Mushrooms are high in vitamins B1, B_2, B_3 and E and zinc. They also contain vitamins C, B_5, B_6 and B12, iron, calcium, chromium, selenium, iodine, phosphorus and potassium. Mushrooms are very tasty by themselves or with other vegetables. They are very "meaty." That's live foods "meaty" and very much appreciated by those who consume them in our social environmental setting.

Mustard greens

All green leafy vegetables are potent body healers in that they rebuild the cell structure of the body. All leafy green vegetables are high in vitamins A, B1, B2, B_3, B_5, B_6, C, E and K, folic acid, choline, fluorine, inositol, PABA, calcium, chlorine, chromium, copper, iodine, iron, silicon, magnesium and manganese. Mustard greens are especially high in vitamins A and B1 and are also a good source of potassium and phosphorus. They have been recommended in cases of anemia, hemorrhoids, constipation, rheumatism and arthritis, to treat kidney and bladder ailments, bronchitis and acidosis and to remove toxins. Mustard greens are also recommended for pregnancy and nursing mothers.

Onion

Onions are a good source of sulfur and potassium. They also contain calcium, chlorine, selenium, phosphorus, iron, inositol, vitamins A, B1, B_2, B_3 and C. (See garlic which has similar properties). Onions are diuretics, laxatives and good antiseptics. They help to drain mucous from the sinuses and cavities and loosen phlegm. Onions are good for the hair, nails and eyes, because of their sulfur content. They are recommended in cases of asthma, bronchitis, pneumonia, influenza, colds and tuberculosis. Onions are also helpful in treating cases of low blood pressure, insomnia, neuritis and vertigo. Because of their antiseptic properties, they can be used to destroy worms and parasites. Onion can be made into a poultice and applied to the chest to treat cases of inflammation of the lungs and applied directly to the skin to treat boils.

Parsley

Parsley is actually declared as an herb but is included here. As I've said, all live foods are actually herbs. It is high in vitamins A, B1, B_2, B_3 and C, calcium, phosphorus and iron. Parsley also contains magnesium, sodium, sulfur, potassium, copper and manganese. Parsley is an excellent blood and body cleanser, cleansing the kidney, the liver and the urinary tract. It is, therefore, helpful in treating acidosis, for removing poisonous drugs from the system, for treating venereal diseases and fever and for bad breath. Parsley is recommended for disorders of the eye and optic nerve, including weak eyes, ulceration of the cornea, cataracts, conjunctivitis and ophthalmia. Parsley improves the metabolism and cell respiration and regeneration. It is helpful in maintaining proper adrenal and thyroid function and for obesity. Parsley is said to promote menstrual discharge and relieve menstrual cramps associated with menstrual irregularities and has been recommended in cases of anemia and high blood pressure as it helps to maintain blood vessels in healthy condition. Parsley is also a diuretic and has been effective for treating accumulation of fluid in body cavities (dropsy). It has also been helpful in cases of inflammation of the kidneys (nephritis), congested liver and gall bladder, for urinary tract diseases and for dissolving kidney and other stones. Parsley has been used to treat rheumatism, arthritis and difficult digestion. In addition, it has been used to treat bronchial and lung disorders, catarrh and tuberculosis. Parsley is an herb and very concentrated; therefore, be careful not to take too much of it alone as this can disarrange the nervous system.

Potato (Sweet)

Sweet potatoes are high in vitamin A, potassium, iron, phosphorus, sulfur and chlorine. They also contain vitamins B1, B_2, B_3, B_5 and C and calcium. Sweet potatoes are helpful for gastric, nerve and muscle disturbances. They are used in treating low blood pressure and poor circulation. Sweet potatoes are easily digestible and thus are recommended for stomach ulcers, inflamed colon, hemorrhoids and diarrhea. They are good cleansers and thus helpful in clearing up skin blemishes. Sweet potatoes have a much higher nutritional value than the Irish or white potato and are good body builders. We assimilate sweet potatoes into our diet through juicing, in salads and, of course, in our very popular living live sweet potato pies.

Radish

Radishes are highest in potassium, sodium, iron and magnesium. They also contain vitamins A, B1, B_2, B_3 and C and phosphorus. They are good for teeth, gums, nerves, hair and nails. Radishes are recommended in cases of nervous exhaustion, constipation, catarrh, obesity, gallstones and tuberculosis. They are diuretics and are good for cleansing, regenerating and restoring the mucous membranes. As with parsley, because radishes are very strong, it is recommended that radish juice be taken with other juices like carrot.

Spinach

All green leafy vegetables are potent body healers in that they rebuild the cell structure of the body. All leafy green vegetables are high in vitamins A, B1, B_2, B_3, B_5, B_6, C, E and K, folic acid, choline, fluorine, inositol, PABA, calcium, chlorine, chromium, copper, iodine, iron, silicon, magnesium and manganese. Spinach is especially high in vitamins A, B_2 and B_5, choline, manganese, potassium, silicon, sodium and chlorine and also contains phosphorus and other minerals. Its vitamin K content makes it helpful in cases of hardening of the arteries, high and low blood pressure, impaired heart function and for hemorrhages, because it aids in the clotting and formation of the blood. Spinach is excellent for cleansing, reconstruction and regeneration of the entire digestive and intestinal tract and it is recommended in treating chronic indigestion and ulcers. Its high calcium content makes it good for strengthening teeth and gums. Spinach is recommended in cases of degeneration of the nerves, nerve exhaustion, neuritis, insomnia, arthritis, obesity, bronchitis, for ailments of the bladder and liver, tumors, thyroid problems, arthritis, abscesses, boils, swelling of the limbs, loss of vigor, rheumatic pains, eye troubles, migraine headaches and constipation as a result of its having laxative properties. Its vitamin E content makes it helpful in preventing miscarriage and treating cases of sterility and impotence. Spinach is also good for the metabolism. Additionally, spinach is an exceptional food for pregnancy as well as an exceptional food to be consumed by nursing mothers.

Spirulina

Spirulina is a complete protein containing all 21 amino acids and is a good source of all of the B complex vitamins, including B12. It is also rich in beta carotene, minerals and essential fatty acids. It is an easily digestible energy source.

Squash, Summer

Summer squash, such as zucchini, is high in inositol and potassium. It also contains vitamins A, B1, B_2, B_3 and C, calcium, iron and phosphorus. It is good for high blood pressure, obesity, constipation, bladder and kidney disorders.

Squash, Winter

Squash is high in Vitamin A and potassium. It also contains vitamins B_1, B_2, B_3 and C, calcium, iron, manganese and phosphorus. It is good for diarrhea, hemorrhoids, inflammation of the colon (colitis), stomach and intestinal ulcers; and kidney, bladder and gall stones. Squash is also good for healthy skin, eyesight and hair.

String Beans

String beans are rich in the B vitamins, calcium, magnesium, phosphorus, potassium, sodium and sulfur. They are good for the skin, hair and nails and for the metabolism. String beans are good for diabetics, because they stimulate pancreas to produce insulin. I've used string bean juice in this manner on various occasions, including with my mother who was a diabetic. After continuous use of string bean juice, her insulin level became so stable that she was taken off of insulin.

Turnip Greens

All green leafy vegetables are potent body healers in that they rebuild the cell structure of the body. All leafy green vegetables are high in vitamins A, B1, B_2, B_3, B_5, B_6, C, E and K, folic acid, choline, fluorine, inositol, PABA, calcium, chlorine, chromium, copper, iodine, iron, silicon, magnesium and manganese. Turnip greens are especially high in vitamin A, sodium, iron, potassium and

94

calcium—containing the highest percentage of calcium of any vegetable. Therefore, they are excellent for the bones and teeth, acidosis, anemia, poor appetite, tuberculosis, obesity, high blood pressure, bronchitis, asthma, liver ailments, gout and bladder disorders. Turnip greens are also a blood purifier, destroying bacterial toxins in the bloodstream. As with all of the dark green leafy vegetables, turnip greens are an excellent food for pregnancy and for nursing mothers. They are also exceptional foods for growing children.

Watercress

Watercress is high in vitamins A and C, fluorine, sulfur, phosphorus, chlorine, potassium, calcium, sodium and magnesium. It also contains vitamins B1, B_2, B_3 and E, folic acid and iron. It is recommended for treating eye disorders, obesity, bleeding gums, arthritis, rheumatism, kidney and liver disorders and dropsy (swelling in body cavities). Watercress stimulates oxygen metabolism, circulatory and heart function and is thus recommended in cases of hardening of the arteries and for menstrual discomfort. Watercress juice is excellent when mixed with other vegetable juices like carrot. One should be careful when consuming watercress juice, because it is known to be a very powerful intestinal cleanser.

Wheatgrass

Wheatgrass is a grass grown from wheat berries. It contains vitamins A, B complex, C and E, calcium, iron, magnesium, potassium and other minerals. Wheatgrass is one of the most potent body healers. It is so potent that herbivorous animals like cows and sheep are able to live solely on wheatgrass indefinitely. Wheatgrass juice is beneficial for the blood, bones, glands, hair, kidneys, liver, muscles, spleen and teeth. It can be applied externally, used as an eyewash or mouthwash, or implanted. Wheatgrass helps to protect against environmental toxins and is a weight-loss aid by stimulating metabolism and suppressing the appetite. According to wheatgrass proponent Ann Wigmore, wheatgrass therapy has cured the following conditions: arthritis, asthma, high blood pressure, boils, Bright's disease, breast cancer, constipation, diabetes, poor eyesight, glaucoma, burns, hair loss, leukemia, migraine headaches, Parkinson's disease, tumors, uterine cancer, obesity and ulcers. Wheatgrass is also said to be helpful for acne and other skin problems, anemia; bone, kidney, liver, bladder and lung disorders; nervous disorders; bronchitis, poor circulation, low blood pressure, heart disease, colitis, eye disorders, hypoglycemia and impotence. Wheatgrass should be consumed in its juice form in small doses or "shots."

Seeds

Seeds are super, super foods. The "nuts" commonly known as almond and cashew nuts are actually fruit-bearing seeds and are included in this section. Seeds are very nourishing in and of themselves. A seed has the capacity to produce a tree that can reproduce itself thousands of times. The fruits of these seeds, like watermelons, are also very special because they can produce in and of themselves whole food nourishment from the seeds that they bear. All seeds are a good source of choline and inositol.

Almonds

Almonds are high in vitamins B1, B_2 and B_3, calcium, iron, inositol, magnesium and phosphorus and also contain vitamin E, biotin, choline, copper, manganese and potassium. Almonds are good for the nerves and are good muscle and body builders. Their calcium content makes them good for building and maintaining healthy teeth and bones.

Cashews

Cashews are very high in vitamins B1 and B_2, iron and phosphorus. They also are a good source of vitamin B_3 and calcium. Cashews are easily digested and are good body builders, helping in cases of emaciation and with problems with the teeth and gums.

Note: It should be noted that there is much discussion about the cashew: it is a wonderful seed that lives very happily at the end of a cashew fruit. In its natural state, it is somewhat gray in color and protected by a very powerful ingredient within the hull of the outer shell of the seed. It can be sun dried and safely removed from its acid-like protective covering, and the tender inner meat will serve its patient consumer a very delicate flavor of tender enjoyment. However, keep in mind that in a commercial-oriented market, the buyers and sellers have no time to wait for a natural solar process, so therefore, they use blow torches and many other fired-up methods of retrieving this very popular seed, and worst of all, they utilize bleach to deceive you into believing that the natural coloration is what you are buying. All in all, if you have the patience and the desire to deal with whole and natural products, then a raw and truly natural cashew will be your priceless reward. If you are blessed to have lived as the I in I did prior to the war in the late '90's in Sierra Leone, you can enjoy the juicy and delicate fruit as well as its delicate seed raw, live and in living color.

Ground Peas (Peanuts)

Peanuts are actually a bean. They are high in vitamins B_3 and B_5, inositol and magnesium. Peanuts also contain significant amounts of vitamins B1, B_2 and E, calcium, iron and potassium. Peanuts are a good body building food and are recommended in cases of under-weight, low blood pressure and weakness.

Pumpkin Seeds (and other squash seeds)

Pumpkin seeds are high in vitamin B_2, iron, phosphorus and zinc and contain significant amounts of inositol and vitamins A, B1 and B_3. They are recommended for prostate problems and for the health of the male hormones. They are also good for constipation and for removal of parasites.

Sesame Seeds (Sesame tahini)

Sesame seeds are an excellent source of calcium, selenium and iron. They are also a good source of vitamins B1, B_2, B_3 and E, magnesium, phosphorous and potassium. Sesame seeds are helpful for constipation, removing pus from the body, chronic skin diseases, swelling and tumors. They are also good for the nerves, heart and liver and for removing intestinal worms. Sesame seeds are good body builders for those who are underweight. The oil can be used to treat burns and skin inflammations and as a hair dressing.

Sunflower Seeds

Sunflower seeds are an excellent source of iron and are also a good source of the B vitamins, particularly B_2 (riboflavin) and calcium. They also contain a significant amount of vitamins A and E and phosphorus. Sunflower seeds are good for weak eyes and dry skin and for building strong nails and teeth. They are also recommended in cases of arthritis. The oil can be used on the skin or as a hair dressing.

Nuts

All nuts are high in vitamins B_6 and E, choline, inositol, magnesium, manganese, phosphorus and copper. They are all good body building and strengthening foods for persons who have low vitality or who are underweight.

Brazil nuts

Brazil nuts are high in calcium, iron, phosphorus and potassium. They also contain vitamin B1. Their calcium content makes them good for teeth and bones. As with all nuts, brazil nuts serve as an excellent food for pregnancy, nursing mothers and for children and growing adults and are good generally for relieving nutritional deficiencies.

Macadamia

Macadamia nuts are high in calcium, phosphorus and iron. They also contain vitamins B1, B_2 and B_3. They are good body builders and helpful for anemia and convalescence.

Pecans

Pecans are high in calcium, potassium, phosphorus and iron. They also contain significant amounts of vitamins A, B1, B_2 and B_3 and small amounts of vitamin C. Pecans are recommended in cases of low blood pressure, weakness and emaciation and for healthy teeth.

Pine nuts

Pine nuts are a good source of vitamins B1, B_2 and B_3, iron and phosphorus and contain significant amounts of vitamin A. Pine nuts are good for body building, strength and energy.

Pistachios

Pistachios contain significant amounts of vitamins A, B1, B_2 and B_3. They are high in protein and are good body builders. Pistachios are good for persons with low blood pressure and low vitality. They help to strengthen teeth and bones and are very tasty when prepared as a nut meat.

Walnuts

Walnuts are a good source of magnesium, B_5 and the other B vitamins, calcium, iron, phosphorus and potassium. They also contain vitamins A, C and E. Walnuts are natural laxatives. They are said to improve the metabolism, strengthen teeth and gums and aid with liver ailments.

Grains

All grains are high in biotin, choline, vitamins B_5, B_6 and E, selenium, magnesium, manganese, chromium and copper. Please refer to *A word about Grains* on page 64 for some important information about selecting grains.

Barley

Barley is high in vitamin B_3 (niacin), phosphorus and iron. It also contains biotin, vitamins B1 and B_2. Barley is good for increasing body weight, relieving stomach ulcers and diarrhea, preventing tooth decay, for hair loss and is good for the nails. It is also recommended in cases of asthma and fever.

Millet

Millet is very high in iron and phosphorus. It is also a good source of vitamins B1, B_2 and B_3 and calcium. Millet is easily digested. It is helpful for constipation and for gaining weight.

Oats

Oats are high in inositol, magnesium, phosphorus, silicon and vitamin K. They also contain a healthy supply of vitamins B1, B_2, B_3 and E, calcium, iron and phosphorus. Oats are good muscle and body builders. They are also good for the glands, teeth, hair and nails.

Quinoa

Quinoa is a good source of iron and contains high levels of potassium and riboflavin, as well as other B vitamins: B_6, niacin and thiamin. It is also a good source of magnesium, zinc, copper and manganese and has significant amounts of vitamin E, folate (folic acid), calcium and phosphorus. Quinoa is a high-protein grain and a good muscle and body builder.

Rye

Rye is a good source of vitamins B1, B_2, B_3 and K, calcium, chromium, iron and phosphorus. It is a good general body and muscle builder and good for the glands.

Wheat

Wheat is a good source of the B-complex vitamins, inositol, vitamin K, phosphorus, iron, selenium, sodium, chromium, calcium and zinc. It is said to be helpful in treating cases of arthritis, rheumatic fever and even cancer. About twenty-five years ago, I took cracked wheat and created a dish similar to rice so as to encourage one of my spiritual mates to consume live foods. This dish was called Kush-Hi Supreme. To this day, that dish, which was a vital part of the *First Innercourse* live foods center in Philadelphia, PA, is a household word for many live foodists. I've also used this dish as a nutritional base for someone who was suffering from cancer. This person later became a very close friend after being cured of cancer through a live foods diet. It must be clearly understood that the base of this dish was organic, raw cracked wheat or quinoa and not bulgur or some other dead and devitalized substance that they call cous cous. It has become very apparent that raw cracked wheat has become very hard to find, with the exception of Arrowhead Mills, on a commercial basis.

Also, be aware that at the time we created kush, we were seen and popularly known for the sundrying process used as part of the preparation procedure. If one is capable of finding organic, freshly-grown wheat or quinoa and sundrying it, one would be very fortunate to enjoy a very wholesome and nutritious meal very similar to the original dish that the I in I created called kush (sometimes mistakenly spelled cush). Keep in mind that the term bulghur wheat is sometimes considered to be a type of wheat, like winter wheat, or a brand. Please be inquisitive about the processing, for many find it easier to "slightly toast" the wheat rather than wait for the sun-drying process.

Another note is to make sure that you always consume any grain fresh from the field while strolling through the grain patch; the fresher the pick, the greater the nutritional capacity and the less the unnecessary starch content that will be consumed. This is why the optimum way to consume grains that you buy or acquire beyond the farm is to sprout them. It is preferable that all grains—such as wheat, oats, barley, rye, or quinoa—be consumed with lots of fresh fruits or vegetables. Soak your grains until sprouting begins, putting back the liquid and life force that has been absorbed during the sundrying process. Make sure that any grain seed that you consume sprouts for optimum nutritional value.

Common Healing Herbs and Spices that Every Live Foodist Should Know

It should be kept in mind that all herbs recommended are prepared by soaking them in spring water or in fresh pressed apple juice at room temperature. Keep in mind that the healing properties of these medicinal herbs are truly released when no heat is applied. This only makes logical sense based on the fact that the live and active enzymes contained in these herbs are best released when the herbs are left in their natural and uncooked state.

Aloe Vera

Aloe Vera is a super body healer and cleanser. It has a tremendous ability to heal wounds and burns and to remove scars. It is also a tremendous internal healer with the capacity to repair damaged tissues. It is also said to be helpful in treating PMS.

Basil

Basil is good for indigestion, fevers, colds, flu, kidney and bladder troubles, headaches, cramps, nausea, vomiting, constipation and nervous conditions. It is

used for relieving gas, reducing fever, as a blood purifier, stimulant and diuretic
and for calming the nerves.

Bay leaves

Bay leaves added to one's food improve flavor and help to improve digestion.
Externally they can be applied as a poultice to the chest for bronchitis and coughs.
Bay leaf infused oil can be applied directly to sprains, for arthritis, rheumatism
and to reduce swelling.

Bilberry

Bilberry is used to strengthen vision and to treat many eye disorders such as night
blindness, macular degeneration*, cataracts, glaucoma and retinopathy. The
leaves have been used to treat adult-onset diabetes and the berries have been used
for diarrhea and dysentery. Bilberry is also helpful for varicose veins.

* The macula is the part of the eye responsible for fine vision. In cases of
macular degeneration, the blood vessels supplying blood to the eye narrow
and harden, causing the tissue to break down. One cause of this condition is
long-term or excessive exposure to ultra-violet and blue light from the sun.
Symptoms of this disorder are: blurry or distorted vision, decreased reading
ability even of large lettering, colors are less bright, there are blind spots
when looking straight ahead, though peripheral vision is still good. Driving
is difficult and vertical lines become wavy. Based on my personal
experience since returning from West Africa, it is my belief that this
condition is caused by ozone depletion. I believe that more and more
individuals living in the Northern Hemisphere will be affected. Being that
it is caused by the breakdown of the ozone layer, we all must be conscious
of using the regenerative herbs that have the regenerative enzymes to
prevent and treat this condition. I have found bilberry to be especially
effective, particularly combined with a live foods diet. This treatment
recommendation is based completely on the premise that one is following a
live foods diet. Affected individuals should purchase special lenses which
block ultra-violet rays at all times and amber or blue-blocking glasses when
in bright sunlight or when driving, to protect their eyes from harmful ultra-
violet rays.

Cayenne Pepper

Cayenne Pepper is considered one of the best blood cleansers in the world. It acts as a stimulant and antiseptic. It relieves gas and bowel pain and prevents and helps with muscle spasms. Cayenne pepper is good for the heart and circulation, and is helpful in treating heart attacks, strokes, hemorrhages, high and low blood pressure, colds, flu, low vitality, headaches, indigestion, depression and arthritis. The powder can be applied to toothaches and inflammations. It can also be used with plantain to draw foreign objects out of the flesh.

Cinnamon

Cinnamon can be used to treat indigestion, gas, chronic diarrhea and dysentery and to relieve gas and bowel pain. It is soothing on damaged and inflamed tissue and has also been helpful in relieving uterine bleeding, cramps, heart and abdominal pain, coughing, wheezing and lower back pain. Cinnamon is a blood cleanser and an excellent seasoning herb, especially with sweet fruits.

Cilantro

A seasoning herb with an excellent taste, particularly when prepared with high-protein dishes like avocado and nuts.

Chamomile

Chamomile is used as a digestive aid and is soothing to the stomach. It also has a calming effect on the nerves and is thus helpful in treating cases of insomnia, irritability and nervousness. Chamomile has also been shown to be effective in relieving menstrual cramps, back and other pain, colds and flu and diarrhea.

Cloves

Cloves increase circulation, improve digestion and are helpful to relieve gas, vomiting and nausea. Chewing cloves relieves toothache pain.

Cumin

Cumin is used to prevent and relieve gas. It has stimulant and antispasmodic (relieves spasms) properties. Cumin is beneficial for the heart and uterus and can be used by lactating women to increases breast milk. It can be applied externally to stimulate local circulation.

Dill

Dill is helpful for colic, stomachaches and pains and indigestion. It is also said to be useful in increasing the breast milk of nursing mothers. The root can be used to treat colds, flu and coughs.

Echinacea

Echinacea is used to treat inflammatory conditions such as boils, skin eruptions, pus-filled sores, venomous bites, gangrene, poison oak, poison ivy, syphilis and gonorrhea and other acute, bacterial or viral infections.

Eyebright

Eyebright can be used to treat diseases of the eye and the sinuses. It may be used as an eyewash.

Ginger

Ginger is a stimulant. It is good for the stomach and intestines and for improving circulation. It is used for easing indigestion, cramps and nausea. Ginger is also helpful in treating colds and flu, coughs, sinusitis and sore throat. It can be made into an oil and applied externally to stiff and inflamed joints and aching muscles or applied to scalp for dandruff. Ginger helps to regulate the menstrual cycle, providing relief from cramping.

Ginseng

Ginseng is beneficial for the heart and for circulation. Thus it is used in cases of high blood pressure, to reduce blood cholesterol and to prevent hardening of the arteries. It also nourishes the blood, making it helpful in treating anemia. Ginseng is beneficial as an overall energy herb and stimulant, useful in treating stress, fatigue and weakness. It is also said to improve memory and to reduce blood sugar levels. Ginseng is nourishing to the male reproductive system, especially red ginseng, which contains testosterone.

Goldenseal

Goldenseal is used to treat inflammatory conditions. It is helpful for acid indigestion, gastritis, colitis, duodenal ulcers, female reproductive disorders, penile discharge, eczema and skin disorders. It dries and cleanses the mucous membranes and is useful in treating liver diseases such as cirrhosis of the liver and hepatitis. This herb should not be taken during pregnancy or by those suffering from hypertension.

Horseheal

Horseheal is a digestive aid, relieving gas. It is also used to treat respiratory problems such as bronchitis and asthma, relieving cough and reducing mucous.

Hibiscus

I have found hibiscus to be a cleansing body tonic. I have also found the hibiscus flower to be very tasty in a salad. We have used this flower to give us an okra-like flavor in certain dishes.

Lemongrass

We have found fresh lemongrass to be very soothing to the nerves. It is also good for treating colds, sore throat and sinus conditions.

Mint

Spearmint and peppermint are useful in treating colds, flu, fever (with chamomile), indigestion, nausea, stomach gas, cramps and spasms. It may also be used with St. John's wort for depression.

Nettles

Nettles is beneficial for the lungs, stomach and urinary tract. It is helpful in treating anemia, for asthma, urinary stones and other urinary complaints, inflammation of the kidneys (nephritis) and inflammation of the bladder (cystitis). Nettles has been used for diarrhea, dysentery, hemorrhoids, arthritis, rheumatism and for treatment of enlarged prostate. Nettles contain vitamin K which helps to reduce internal and external bleeding. Nettle root stimulates white blood cell production. It can also be applied to the scalp to stimulate hair growth.

Nutmeg

In small doses, nutmeg can be taken for chronic nervous disorders and heart problems. In large doses, nutmeg can be harmful and can cause miscarriage.

Raspberry leaves

Red raspberry leaf is recommended for menstrual cramps and excessive menstrual bleeding, preventing miscarriage and for easing childbirth. It helps to prevent infection and to tighten tissue and stimulates contractions during labor. It is rich in calcium, magnesium and iron. Red raspberry is also good for fevers and to reduce bleeding.

Rosemary

Rosemary is good for relieving headaches. It is also helpful for indigestion, colic, nausea, gas and fever. Rosemary is good for the hair and scalp and can be steeped in spring water and applied as a hair rinse after shampooing.

Sage

Sage is useful in slowing the secretion of fluids and is therefore helpful in relieving night sweats, clearing vaginal discharge and reducing/stopping the production of breast milk. Sage is also beneficial for diarrhea, dysentery, colds, flu, sinus congestion, bladder infections and inflammatory conditions. It can be gargled to relieve sore throat and mouth.

St. John's Wort

St. John's Wort is used to treat pains and diseases of the nervous system including anxiety, depression, neuralgia (nerve pain), rheumatism and arthritis.

Senna

Senna is a laxative used to treat acute constipation. It is not recommended during pregnancy.

Strawberry leaves

Strawberry leaves can be used to treat kidney ailments and diabetes.

Thyme

Thyme is beneficial for removing parasites and intestinal worms. It is also helpful for bronchitis, whooping cough and laryngitis. Thyme can also be used to relieve diarrhea, gastritis and to improve appetite. Its antiseptic properties make it useful as a mouthwash and body cleanser. It can be applied to fungal infections like athlete's foot and to skin parasites.

Turmeric

Turmeric is a blood purifier which is used to heal wounds, relieve pains in limbs, break up congestion and as a restorative after blood loss from child birth. It is good for blood circulation, regulating menstruation, relieving cramps and PMS, reducing fever and for nosebleeds. Turmeric promotes digestion and assimilation and is an anti-inflammatory, making it good for soothing bruises and injuries. It is also said to reduce blood sugar levels, to prevent and dissolve gallstones and to be beneficial in treating hepatitis.

Divine Clarity, Revisited

We hope the spirit of divine clarity has guided you into the sacred reality that organically whole live fruits, vegetables, seeds, nuts and grains, herbs and spices are, in fact, the supreme holistic living foods for human consumption. Being the most holy and divine foods of the Divine Children of the Sun and their offspring, we also hope that you have begun to understand that your mind of thought has been baptized in lies and confusion in order to turn you into a hapless and hopeless consumer. Hapless in that you wander around in a psychedelic maze of confusion turning illusions into fantasies and fantasies into illusions, accepting and worshipping the deceit regarding dead and devitalized foods and other products—deceit that declares these satanically vicious and deadly lies as truth even though your mind of thought, your body of flesh and your sacred spirit scream for mercy from their painfully fatal and destructive consequences. Hopeless in the sense that there is absolutely no hope of your enjoying anything, but a cultural norm of lust, lies, illusions, confusion, conflict and deadly destruction throughout this facade of life that your acts and behaviors have actually declared as a systematic trip leading deeper into death. Your only hope is that you will be able to buy enough things, that you will have a well-attended funeral with lots of flowers and things and that you will be welcomed in heaven or hell after you die.

Imagine a manufacturer taking some whole grain, deep frying it into some substance called wheat flakes and then telling the consumer that, although all of the life force has been roasted and toasted out of it, it has been "fortified" with the identifiable essential vitamins that were originally in it and which were definitely murdered. Please remember that, initially, they were selling this item to you without fortifying it and then, after the USDA was forced to acknowledge the unhealthy method of preparing these items, a new trick of fortification was invented. Please, someone tell me how, in and of itself, you can pull Vitamin B out of the body of a living thing and then tell me how you can take that Vitamin B and reinsert it back into this dead and devitalized commodity, place it on a shelf and expect it to stay alive until someone buys and crunches on this useless substance as his or her breakfast meal.

I hope that some kind of divine clarity will allow you to understand that there are key words used that will automatically tell you that there is a lie in the game that will prevent you from having a whole relationship with that commodity. Key words like supplement. How are you going to supplement the real thing? Supplement means that the real thing is not there, so they're going to add something to it, or give you something to replace the real thing that should have been left there in the first place. For example, when you cook some spinach, you're preparing a major sin and major consequences for your body. After you've cooked out the vitamin B and most likely everything else, the concept is to take a vitamin or mineral supplement and fulfill your dead and devitalized taste buds while getting supplemental nourishment. Why not get the real, whole, live thing from the beginning, plus all of the vital and unidentifiable life substances within the food which biochemists and others have yet to isolate, identify, or understand?

What the manufacturers and biochemists are trying to tell you is that they've become as powerful as god and that they have the ability to extract the particular vitamin necessary. This idea adds to the whole game of lies and illusions, because once they come up with the concept that you can get all of the Vitamin B that you need in one pill, a new fad is created and a massive consumption of that commodity takes place; because there are so many people looking for a quick fix. Please let me remind you that the normal case is that the fad ends when it is realized that the new supplement that was invented to replace the original substance that was taken out has created a new cancer which did not exist before these new inventions which were made for social economic gain. These wonderful inventions are mass produced to create social economic gains off of a people too ignorant to ask the common sense questions.

What has happened is that food, one of our most basic needs, has become a major profit industry. Quick, fast, convenient, dead and devitalized food substances are massively manufactured and distributed in whatever manner necessary to make the most money in the shortest period of time while spending the least. If you are not getting all of your nutrients from your food, then don't worry. There's a pill or supplement that will "replace" whatever was lost in the manufacturing process, or so you will be told. And if the supplement creates a new problem, there will be a new pill to supplement the supplement. All of these quick, fast, convenient, dead and devitalized food substances and supplements are massively consumed by individuals who are spending the vast majority of their time working for a dollar to spend on more and more dead, devitalized and useless convenience products all because they don't have time to grow, buy, or prepare the real, whole, natural and live thing. They don't have time, because they've gone off on a shopping spree to buy the latest commodity to replace the old one that they bought last week which is still working quite well. Or they are at the hospital, the psychiatrist's office, or bedridden at home, trying to recuperate from insanity gone mad as a result of the massive consumption of dead and devitalized foods, their fortifications and supplements. A large majority of this group find themselves in the mortuary sooner than they expected.

In case you still don't understand what's going on, the basic concept that the food and supplement manufacturers are telling you is that a little of something is better than nothing at all. If you don't understand the meaning of "A little something is better than nothing at all," it means that what the biochemists and others are telling you is that the dead and devitalized foods that you are eating are basically like eating nothing at all. Therefore, you need loads of supplemental vitamins. It is also a play on your intelligence, because what it is saying is that you lack the true will power to make wholesome decisions about what you consume. In real terms, it also indicates that you are so addicted to dead and devitalized foods that you are incapable of doing without them, regardless of the aches, pains and death that they cause you, your friends and your so-called loved ones. As most junkies tend to do, you prefer to replace one problem with another problem instead of dealing with a divine solution. If that's where you are, it is probably no good for you to read any further. The best thing for you to do is to turn on some Jerry Springer reruns or the news and enjoy another glorious day of conflict and confusion before you go to the church, synagogue or mosque this weekend. Don't forget your popcorn, corn chips and pasteurized, "natural" fruit beverage that has been fortified with Vitamin C. And whether or not you are a vegan who is eating all of that dead and devitalized stuff, you may as well take home a bucket of Kentucky Fried or have a Big Mac attack with your salad. For the rest of you who are feeling the divine vibration, we can go on and discuss the quickest and most effective way to cleanse the toxins from the body and the mind and to rebuild the temple of the spirit.

CHAPTER 7: JUICING

In Chapter 6, we explored some of the basic elements of foods which have been scientifically identified and classically accepted as needed by the body. We further identified the divine foods of the trees of life which definitely have these elements. It is also a known factor and must be clarified at this point in time, that there are thousands of trace elements that have not even been identified yet, trace elements that can only be found in live foods. No matter how much time scientists spend in the lab for centuries to come, it will still equate to the fact that no part or sum of parts is greater than its whole. That is to say that the life element of food and the life element of the body requires whole and live active enzyme relationships in order to be completely wholesome. These elements are and will continue to be, beyond the ability of science to isolate, define and/or comprehend in a piecemeal manner. For example, algebraically $a + b + c + d$=spinach or H_2O is water. But neither H nor O by themselves or taken together in the wrong combination with a supplement is equal to water. Just try drinking some H_2O_2, or hydrogen peroxide and witness the consequences. By the way, make sure you have another person standing nearby to be a witness, just in case you take too much.

I ask you to now join me in a glorious journey deep into the Most Supreme Spirit of Love, Righteousness and the Holistic Living Truth About Supreme Love. Where should we begin? Well, it's quite obvious that if we are taking a journey so glorious that we will need the most glorious and highest-octane mental, physical and spiritual fuel available in order to complete this mission successfully. Added to this prerequisite is the fact that we have an extremely urgent and dire emergency facing us on the crust of the planet. Recognizing that, it is also extremely obvious that we must take the most urgent actions to correct this most urgent and dire emergency facing the sacred sons and daughters of Man. So, what are the foods that will be able to nourish the body as quickly and as urgently as possible, while at the same time cleansing the body of the dead and toxic debris with which it has been filled and repairing it of the tremendously devastating damage that it has endured?

The live foods for human consumption are whole fruits, vegetables, seeds, nuts and grains. Our mission in this chapter is to deal with the most expedient method of assimilating these foods into the body. When we say assimilate into the body, I hope that everyone understands that the body has a special river that flows from the tip top of the head to the bottom of the toe. That river is called the blood/circulatory system. Therefore, it should be very clear that under any dire emergency, the quicker we can get whole, live, life enzymes into the bloodstream, the quicker we will be able to address any problem that the body may have in cleansing and/or healing itself.

When consuming live fruits, vegetables, seeds, nuts and grains, the most expedient way of getting those whole foods into the body with the least amount of tax on the body is through whole and live juicing. When I say juicing, it is extremely important to recognize that we are talking about extracting every inch of liquid content from the particular fruit or vegetable so as to formulate a live and wholesome food that we call juice. In order to do that, the first thing that is necessary is to be able to obtain or create the proper kind of juice extracting mechanism. The ideal situation is to take a press that has no relationship with heat whatsoever and to have the juices extracted through the use of pressure. The extraction must be whole and complete in order to obtain whole and complete nourishment from the juicing process. After obtaining the proper kind of extraction mechanism, you are now on the road to a completely unique experience in whole health.

Equipment

Juicers

If this Divine Child of the Sun were going out today to obtain the most efficient juicing equipment for my family and me, the specifications of that mechanism would be of the same kind and type as the Norwalk juicer with a few personal alterations. Since the Norwalk juicer is available in a home model, it is the juicer that I would recommend as an investment for any serious live foodist. For those of you who are not quite prepared to pay several thousand dollars or more for a hydraulic press juicer, there is a viable alternative for your money. Any serious look at the market will let you know that the most viable alternative for your money is the Champion juicer. Its shortcoming is that it does get warm, but overall, it will provide you with excellent juice that is well extracted. Both the Norwalk and the Champion are masticating juicers. They masticate the fruit or vegetables into a paste, and the juice is squeezed out through a screen at the bottom of the juicer. The Norwalk juicer includes a second step to the process by ejecting the masticated fruit and/or vegetable paste into a bag which is then hydraulically pressed to obtain the maximum amount of juice. The Champion juicer costs about $250 to $300.

It is not our business, really, to disturb the economic advancement of any company, but we do recommend that anyone who is serious about obtaining optimal nutrition from your juice use centrifugal juicers as his or her last alternative. Centrifugal juicers chop the fruit and/or vegetables being juiced, spinning them at high speed to separate the juice from the pulp. We have found that these juicers tend to allow too much oxidation. This means that vital oxygen within the food is lost during the juicing process because of the vacuum that is created during the spinning process.

Wheatgrass juicers

For things like wheatgrass, other leaves and sprouts, I would recommend that one buy a wheatgrass juicer. What is available is a manual type, or if you are a bit lazy, there is an electrical model available. I don't know if there are other models available, but the manual that looks like a grinder makes excellent juice, especially when the screws are tight and you can always put the "pulp" through a second time to extract more juice. The manual wheatgrass juicer costs approximately $75.

Citrus juicers

For oranges, grapefruits, limes and lemons, it is advisable that you buy yourself a good citrus juicer. These juicers range from the large, manual stainless steel type to the small hand-size manual type. We recommend the Hamilton Beech stainless steel, hand-pressed citrus juicer. It has a long handle and gives you a lot of pressure on your juicing. This should run you about $100 to $130. Avoid the type of juicer that has alloyed metals, because it will destroy essential vitamins in your juices. There are also some smaller, plastic models which cost less and do a whole lot less juicing. The most ideal kind of juicer would be one made of hard wood. Keep your eye out. We will probably come out with one.

Blenders

Since you will most likely find occasions to blend things like bananas and soaked seeds and nuts into your juices for live smoothies, etc., it is advised that you buy yourself a very good blender—something like a Kitchen Aid or an Osterizer. We have found them to be dependable and they have provided us with excellent usage. We recommend the one with the glass bowl, because it is easier to clean. A good blender will cost you around $100.

Regarding equipment, please keep in mind that the Vitamix is an expensive blender, not a juicer. When looking for equipment, one should try one's best to locate the commercial model, because you are going to be doing a lot of juicing.

Now that we have all of our equipment lined up and ready to use, let's move on. The Kwatamani Family Community's live foods approach is to view all foods as the holistic living medicine for the body, the brain and the spirit. Looking at it as such, let us understand that there is one kind of medicine for cleansing and another for building and repairing the whole body system. The live foods medicines for cleansing, basic and simple, are fresh fruits. Fresh, live, whole, organic fruits. The live foods for repairing are just as simple, fresh vegetables. Fresh, live, whole, organic vegetables. When we want this cleansing and repairing healing process to take place as quickly as possible, the best method to use is live juicing. Fresh, live, wholesome, organic juicing. Below are some juices and juice combinations that are very popular with the I in I, juices that I'm sure will greatly assist you in your divine mental, physical and spiritual development.

Fruit Juices:

Coconut Water

coconut

Take fresh coconut and bust it open, being careful not to spill any of the water inside. Pour off water into a glass and drink.

This is an excellent tonic if you want to get the electrical energy force of the body really moving while flushing the system. The electromagnetic force in coconut water is just as complete and powerful as coconut water is a complete and whole food.

Mango Nectar

mangoes

Wash fruit. Slice fruit into chunks, taking care not to waste the juice. Remove and discard the seed(s). Juice and serve.

You may juice the skin. Some delicious variations are ...

Mango Coconut

mango nectar
coconut water

Blend/mix ingredients and serve.

Sweet Sweet Mango

mango nectar
sugar cane

Cut off desired amount of sugar cane. Peel sugarcane. Slice sugar cane into chunks. Juice sugarcane. Blend/mix sugarcane juice with mango nectar. Enjoy!

Piña Colada

coconut
pineapple

Bust coconut. Pour off coconut water and save to drink later. Remove hard coconut from shell. Rinse coconut and slice into small chunks. Set aside. Peel pineapple, removing leaves and skin. Slice into chunks. Juice coconut chunks until you have the desired amount of milk. Coconut pulp/chaff can be discarded eaten over puddings, sprinkled over live cookies or kwakies as we call them, or stuffed inside of a juicy medjool date. Juice pineapple chunks. Combine pineapple juice and coconut milk. Serve and drink.

For another variation of this exotic and delicious live juice, you can blend in a banana!

Citrus Max

orange
grapefruit
lemon and/or lime

Rinse fruit. Slice into halves. For a sweeter juice, use more oranges than grapefruits. Juice oranges and grapefruits. Combine. Add lemon and/or lime to taste.

Live Champagne

champagne grapes

Wash grapes. Remove grapes from stem. Juice and serve.

Watermelon Juice

watermelon

Slice melon into thick strips a few inches long for easier juicing. Juice melon strips, seeds and all. This delicious and refreshing juice is wonderful for your kidneys and bladder.

Apple Ginger

apple
gingerroot

Rinse fruit and ginger. Slice apple(s) into eighths. Slice off chunks of ginger to suit your taste. (Remember, it has a bite). Juice apples and ginger chunks. Strain and serve for a spicy and tasty drink that is good for fighting off sore throats and colds.

Berry Delicious

berries of choice e.g. strawberries, blueberries ...

Rinse berries. Juice and serve.

These juices are very concentrated, though absolutely delicious. We recommend that they be taken in small quantities or combined with other juices.

Cantaloupe

cantaloupe

Slice cantaloupe in half. Remove seeds. Slice cantaloupe into chunks. Juice and serve.

You can also juice honeydew or other melons.

Peach Nectar

peaches

Wash fruit. Slice fruit into chunks, taking care not to waste the juice. Remove and discard the seed(s). Juice and serve.

Vegetable Juices:

Supreme Green

spinach
kale
parsley
turnip greens
mustard greens

Rinse vegetables. Slice off tough stems. Juice greens. Combine and serve.

This juice is packed with super supreme greens and loads of vitamin A, iron, calcium and other minerals. A wonderful tonic for the teeth, bones, blood and eyes.

Orange Power

sweet potato
carrot

Wash vegetables. Slice sweet potato into chunks. Remove tips and tops from carrots. Juice carrots and sweet potato chunks. Strain and serve.

This sweet juice is a powerhouse of vitamin A, making it a great tonic to strengthen the eyes, genito-urinary system, the gastrointestinal tract and a great infection fighter.

Spinach Apple

spinach
apples

Wash vegetables/fruit. Slice apple(s) into eighths. Juice vegetables/fruit. Strain. Combine and serve.

This juice is an excellent blood builder and is particularly recommended for pregnant women for its high iron and calcium content. It helps to prevent bone loss and anemia during pregnancy.

Spinach Carrot

spinach
carrots

Wash vegetables/fruit. Remove tops and tips from carrots. Slice apple(s) into eighths. Juice vegetables/fruit. Strain. Combine and serve.

Like the above combination, this juice is excellent for both pregnant and nursing women.

Carrot Apple Parsley

carrots
apple(s)
parsley

Wash vegetables/fruit. Remove tops and tips from carrots. Slice apple(s) into eighths. Juice vegetables/fruit. Strain. Combine and serve.

This juice is a cleansing drink and is good for improving eyesight, aiding digestion, strengthening the skin, hair and nails; and fighting infection.

Cool Tomato

tomato
mint

Wash tomatoes and mint leaves. Slice tomato into chunks. Juice tomatoes and mint.

This live, refreshing juice is high in natural organic calcium, sodium, potassium, magnesium and vitamin C.

Eye Tonic

carrots
bilberries
parsley

Wash carrots, parsley and berries. Remove tops and tips from carrots. Juice fruits/vegetables. Combine and serve.

This juice is an excellent tonic for improving eyesight and treating eye disorders.

Look at the vegetable list, select from the vegetables listed and combine them in any manner that you wish depending on your concerns and nutritional needs and tastes.

Smoothies and other blends:

Apple Almond

apples
almonds (pre-soaked)

Wash apples. Slice apples into eighths. Juice apples. Strain juice and place it in blender. Drain off soaking water from almonds and discard. Rinse almonds. Place almonds in blender. Blend until smooth. Serve.

Apple Banana

apple
banana

Wash your fruit. Juice apple(s). Strain apple juice to remove any remaining pulp. Take the strained juice and place it in the blender with banana(s). Blend. Serve and drink.

This is a good high-energy juice for when you are feeling slow and sluggish. For extra energy add medjool dates to taste.

Apple Strawberry

Apple(s)
Strawberries

Wash fruit. Slice apple(s) into eighths. Rinse berries. Juice apple slices. Put apple juice into blender. Add strawberries. Blend and serve.

You can also juice the strawberries. Try this one with fresh blueberries, cherries, or raspberries or a berry combination for variety.

Manpower

apples
banana(s)
pumpkin seeds (presoaked)

Wash apples. Slice apples into eighths. Juice apples. Strain juice and place it in blender. Drain off soaking water from pumpkin seeds and discard. Rinse seeds. Add banana and pumpkin seeds to blender. Blend until smooth. Serve.

For another variation of this drink, try substituting sunflower seeds for the pumpkin seeds.

"Chocolate" Milk

coconut
raw carob powder

Bust coconut, being careful not to spill the water inside. Pour off coconut water and put it to the side. Remove hard coconut from shell. Cut coconut into small chunks. Rinse coconut chunks to remove debris. Juice coconut chunks. Place juiced coconut milk into blender. Add carob powder to taste. Blend and serve.

Orange Banana

oranges
banana(s)

Rinse oranges. Slice them into halves and juice. Place orange juice in blender. Add banana(s). Blend and serve. To spice this combination up, you can add a little juiced ginger.

CHAPTER 8: LIVE FOODS (FOR YOUR INFORMATION)

Transitioning to a Live Foods Diet

The best way make a complete and whole transition to a live foods diet is to begin urgently and immediately to eat only whole, live fruits, vegetables, seeds, nuts and grains. This means that you must make a complete mental transition, physical transition and spiritual transition. In order to transition to a live foods diet, the spirit must be awakened with enough surging strength and power to communicate to the brain the Supreme Spirit of Love for the whole essence. Once the spirit has been awakened with the necessary degree of strength and power, one has the spiritual will to be able to make the mental transition of actually physically changing one's diet. The awakening of spirit occurs when the mind of thought reaches to the level and degree that it is inclined to research, analyze and reason with the Most Supreme Spirit of Love, Righteousness and the Holistic Living Truth About Supreme Love. Let me make one point clear; mental reasoning that will cause divine change just does not occur unless there is some type of shock wave. This is especially true in an environment that perpetuates deceitful attitudes, behaviors and ways of life where contradictory life patterns are a norm.

When I say shock wave, what I mean is that a person with a severe case of cancer tends to have enough fear for his or her life to immediately begin to research alternative cures, especially if he or she has had the experience of seeing individuals use conventional cures with little or no success. This occurs even more so when the conventional medical establishment has told that individual that he or she has little or no chance of survival except through a process of chemotherapy—which will only extend that individual's life for a short, designated period of time. I have had the responsibility of having someone in that situation come to me in the past, and after explaining to him how the defense immunity system of the body works and how the cell structure is completely dependent on live life enzymes for reproduction and rejuvenation, the individual immediately changed to a live foods diet. For an extensive period of time, this diet consisted solely of live juices and some of the most bitter, nasty-tasting live herbs on the planet. This individual adhered to this diet with a smile, especially after living past the period of time that he was told that he was not supposed to ever live to see. In his particular case, the spirit was inspired enough to communicate to the brain, and the brain responded to the divine communications of the spirit with enough submission to save the life of the temple of that spirit. This gave that spirit a greater strength to continue its supreme journey forward without being trapped in a dead and devitalized prison, which is what occurs when the brain is too defunct to carry out the divine messages of the spirit.

I've also had the unfortunate responsibility of dealing with another individual who had cancer. This particular individual sought the I in I out because of my reputation for healing through live foods. The particular individual, after taking more than ample of my precious time, decided definitely to change her diet. But, in that decision, she decided to delay it until after a well-established end-of-the-year holiday feasting period. The unfortunate thing about this individual, as sweet and as beautiful as she was, was that she actually had her last supper, both literally and figuratively and never had the chance to change on the date that she had designated as her live foods, changeover date. Within a short span of time, her body deteriorated so rapidly that she died. It is my belief that had she taken direct and immediate action to urgently consume fresh, whole, organic live foods, as prescribed in this book, she would still be around today. In this case, her spirit suffered from the delayed reaction of the brain, which took life, and the presence of time surrounding life, for granted.

It is very important that I make something very clear at this point. The holistic living truth is that the spirit is the essence of our life form and of our existence. The body is the temple of our essence. The brain is the controller of the central nervous system and the mind of thought. When the brain is in divine harmony, it takes all instructions directly from the spirit and nowhere else. This is a state of being that can only occur in one living a divine holistic living way of life. And, even in that case, it requires a tremendous amount of divine surrender to the supreme principles of Love, Righteousness and the Holistic Living Truth About Supreme Love. In essence, it requires that one adhere to the principles and practices of living in divine oneness with the universe of the Most High; however, the divine communications between the brain and the spirit can be disrupted by the energy of deceit.

If you expect to have a lively, wholesome, loving, divine and sacred spirit, then you must put in lively, wholesomely divine and sacred foods. Let's take this from a mathematical perspective, using someone who says that they eat a 50% live foods diet as an example. If you take a positive 9 (+9)—call this live and whole foods—and then take a negative (-9) as dead and devitalized foods and you add these together, what's the result? If you add a positive nine to a negative nine, the result is zero. The answer is not 50/50, the answer is 0 (zero), because you have actually depleted the positive factors in your body by adding the negative of the dead and devitalized foods. If you add the negative factors of dead and devitalized, processed and artificially flavored and colored foods, you have actually circumvented all of the positive life force energies of that live and wholesome food. It should now be clear that a diet of 100% whole, live, fresh and organic fruits, vegetables, seeds, nuts and grains is divinely required in order to elevate your mental, physical and spiritual essence to divine oneness and that sacred and holistic living way of life that will enable you to transition into a more wholesome, healthy and enjoyable lifestyle. It should also be clear that there is absolutely no time to delay in making a whole and complete transition to a 100% live foods diet or to play with the deceitful idea of eating 50% live, 75% live, mostly live or any variation thereof.

Life is a present situation that we must face on a daily basis with each occurrence. In facing that, we must realize what the whole concept of Supreme Love, Righteousness and the Holistic Living Truth About Supreme Love is all about. The concept that represents that most supreme energy of the Most High, the Most Supreme and Holy Spirit of the Almighty God. That particular concept that represents KWA TA MAN I, the Most Supreme and Holy Spirit of the Almighty God will, in fact, make it very clear that when we say we have a love for ourselves, we must play that love out supremely and divinely through a holistic living diet. A holistic living diet consists of live, whole, nutrients at their most optimal level possible if we have the highest level of love for ourselves. To do anything else is a statement of the lack of love, care and appreciation that we have for ourselves, the Most High and any one of our kind upon this planet, as well as any offspring that we may produce. To deplete the mental, physical and spiritual self through a negative diet, a diet of death and devitalization is a statement of a lack of self-esteem. It's a statement of a lack of self-love. It's a statement of a lack of a supreme ideology for the self and for those whom the self may bring forward and encounter. In fact, to make the statement, "I love myself" is simple and easy to make, because words can be spouted by anyone. But to say "I love myself" through the divine acts and requirements of consuming a live and holistic living diet, a live diet of the holy fruits of the trees of life, is the most divine and sacred act of stating the love that one has for oneself, the love that one has for any offspring that one may bring forward and the most supreme and sacred love that one has for the Most High.

Since we are clearly saying that if you have any love for yourself, you will immediately change your diet to a 100% live diet, you may be asking why we even use the word "transition" to describe this process of changing the diet. When we use the word transition, we are not speaking of the process of changing your diet. This should be instant. When we speak of transitioning, we are specifically speaking of the process that the body goes through when a person changes his or her diet from one of dead and devitalized foods to a completely live diet. While there is no question that the healthiest and sanest thing to do is to go 100% live immediately, your body will experience some discomfort as a result. This does not mean that live foods do not agree with you or that live foods are making you sick!!! The change in diet will set in motion a healing, cleansing and rebuilding process as your body rids itself of the toxins that have accumulated in your system for however many years you have been consuming dead and devitalized, artificially flavored, colored and preserved food substances. No act or deed or even thought is without consequences. The consequences of your way of life have actually become a part of your cell structure.

That is to say, only you know how many years, you have been consuming dead and devitalized foods. Added to that, your parents before you consumed dead and devitalized foods. At this point, it begins to become a part of your DNA, as your genes begin to mutate from a disassociation with the live characteristics of living foods. Obviously the only way to change the genetic mutation of degeneration will be to change the living attitudes and behaviors of how you eat, drink and spiritually relate. Although you are now making a change, honorably, wholly and sincerely, it must be clear that you must pay the consequences for the truth that you have rejected all of these years and, sadly, for the holistic living truth that was rejected before you. However, it is better to stop all of the madness right now and suffer from boils, cysts, diarrhea, pus-filled lesions on the skin, ringworm and other fungal skin infections, headaches, yeast infections, weight loss and having lumps of clotted mass come out of the bowels that was more than likely cancer waiting to happen. Although these reactions tend to come swiftly and quickly, the majority do not seem to last long, especially if you are eating whole and properly and flushing your system. As we said earlier, the system requires cleansing, flushing and rebuilding. Clearly the rebuilding process is the process which requires the greatest amount of time. It is quite normal for the rebuilding process to take as long as a full seven years.

It takes seven years for the body to rebirth itself. That is to say, it takes seven years for the entire cell system of the body to be totally reborn. The process is ongoing. Although the process is ongoing, the whole system does not complete itself for a period of seven years. When I say it takes seven years for the body to go through a full rebirth from the outer to the innermost cell, I am not saying that after seven years your body is completely healed of all ills. In actually, the length of time of a full, absolute and total healing depends on the amount of damage that has been done to the body and the amount of time that this damage has been consistently applied to the body.

Therefore, the death and the stench of the impurities from the toxic waste that you consumed five years ago, still remains in your body as pus, mucous and rotten infestation immersed and locked in the cell structure of your colon and the other vital parts of your body. This infestation has been gathered together within the fatty tissue, dirty lungs, the intestinal colon, the brain cells, the lymph and the arteries and is expressed in chronic and fatal diseases such as high and low blood pressure, heart attacks, ulcers, mental illness, stress, cancer, diabetes and AIDS. This infestation must come out of the body in order for you to have a wholesome and healthy existence. Believe it or not, only live life enzymes have the whole capacity to rid your body of the devastating blows of death and deadly destruction. The cell structures of the body must be reborn of whole and live foods in order for you to rejuvenate your holy temple that is called the body of flesh. Let's keep in mind that when we say the body of flesh, we are including the brain as part of that body. When we say the brain, we are talking about the energy of thought that is reasoning, memory and analysis. That energy of thought is the mind of thought. Therefore, when we say the brain, let's make it very clear that we are talking about the mind of thought.

We specifically wanted to make clear this information about the brain, as part and parcel of the body of flesh. The major difference between the brain and the body is that the brain cells do not replenish themselves. Therefore, it is imperative that you eat at the most wholesome level possible, *i.e.* a holistic live foods diet. One may reason that the brain has millions and millions or billions of live life cells, so why worry? But once a brain cell dies, it can never be replenished or replaced. Especially since the average person only uses a small portion of the brain's live life power and ability. This is a great rationale if you wish to keep yourself limited regarding holistic and divine communications with the inner spirit. It's also a great rationale if you feel satisfied and tickled too about today's, present-day attitudes and behaviors that are infesting the globe with death and deadly deceit. However, if you have any idea about establishing, maintaining and sustaining a holistic living way of life mentally, physically and spiritually, it behooves you to master the divine methods of maintaining and preserving the life of every single brain cell available.

Clearly this tremendous live life organ of the central nervous system, which houses billions of highly-energized live life cells, is very much misunderstood. There seems to be a tremendous misunderstanding as to the divine necessity of the sacred electrical forces that come from live, whole foods. There seems to be a misunderstanding regarding the abilities of these live whole living foods to connect the whole mind of thought of the brain to the supreme essence of the holy spirit within. As a matter of fact, it has become clear to the I in I, that the vast majority of the bodies of flesh that are now walking the planet Earth are being totally and absolutely controlled by the energies of deceit and self destruction, as opposed to being controlled by the supreme holy spirit within. This is a very serious conversation, with a very serious message that is extremely important at this time of the gathering of the Divine and Sacred Few. Make no mistake about it. In this time of extreme corruption and excessive deceit and deadly destruction, one needs every single live life cell possible to be totally and absolutely in tune with the holistic living vibration of the holy spirit within.

What live foods do is give you that extra burst of divine energy where you need it the most. That is, live foods supply you with the supreme fuel to divinely expedite supreme reasoning and supreme analysis within the mind of thought. Live foods have the living cell power and ability to reunite the life cell structure of the mind of thought of the brain, the most supreme essence of the spirit. Without the consumption of live whole fruits, vegetables, seeds, nuts and grains, one can automatically expect to perpetuate negative, mutated and self-destructive responses from a brain that is automatically cut off from its living relationship with the sacred holy spirit within. Thus, a malnourished, dead and devitalized diet automatically prohibits divine mental, physical and spiritual growth and development regardless of the rhetoric perpetuated, the excuses, the religious doctrine, or the social order to which one belongs. I hope that this will allow each and every reader to understand why the concept that you are what you eat is divinely equal to the concept that if you eat dead, you will think dead thoughts and perform deadly behaviors. And that the sum total of these two statements is directly proportionate to the concept of life to life and death to death.

I also hope that these very vital points will allow any individual presently having difficulties rejecting and moving away from a dead and devitalized way of thinking, eating and behaving to realize that your difficulties rest in the fact that your brain does not have a divine connection with your spirit, because the foods that you have been consuming are cooked, processed, dead and devitalized. I also hope that you understand that this modern social economic environment is not aimed at empowering your spirit with the divine and sacred will over your brain, for to do so would completely alter the economics and financial abilities of those who are in control of the social environment. If your spirits were empowered with the holy will to consume live foods, wealth would be empowered in the hands of divine agriculture. There would be no need to murder animals for shoes and clothing and to satisfy your taste buds. We would rather deal with natural manufacturing processes with fibers and materials from alternative materials. We would make much better use of our natural resources and it would be much less wasteful of the sacred gifts given to us on this planet. There would be no place for stoves and, of course, there would be a tremendous alteration of the various food markets so as to truly address foods that we need instead of devitalized substances of foods that we have learned to want and desire for suicidal reasons.

I hope that we now have a better understanding about the body, the cells of the body and the usage and replenishing process. I hope that this analysis has made it much clearer as to why the first divine act and requirement is that the sacred sons and daughters consume live, whole, divine fruits, vegetables, seeds, nuts and grains. I hope that it is also very clear that, before you truly have a right to speak against live foods: live fruits, vegetables, seeds, nuts and grains, nature's divine requirements as a divine law is that you must consume live foods for seven consecutive holistic living years before you actually have a right to speak against it. Nature also gives the supreme guarantee that your whole life—your mental, physical and spiritual existence upon this planet—will change you divinely and beyond recognition. This is the holistic living truth about Supreme Love, and it is absolutely imperative that you live according to the principles of Supreme Love, Righteousness and the Holistic Living Truth About Supreme Love or suffer the most painful, devastating, disenchanting and deadly consequences.

CHAPTER 9: INTRODUCTORY RECIPES TO GET YOU STARTED

We are sure that you will find, in transitioning to a live foods diet that your taste buds will begin to alter. When consuming a dead and devitalized diet, the taste buds become dulled by excessive salt, artificial flavors, artificial colors, additives, preservatives, processed starches and flours, cooked foods and excess and artificial sugars in the diet. As you become accustomed to consuming only live and whole foods, your natural taste buds will become enhanced, and you will develop a deep love and appreciation for fresh, live and whole fruits, vegetables, seeds, nuts and grains in their raw, living and natural state.

Our approach to food preparation is that all foods and meals are combined and prepared for maximum digestibility and nutritive value. Rather than giving you a list of recipes with measurements and minutia, our purpose is to equip you with the knowledge and basic understanding of the foods and how they are best combined for maximum health and flavor. This information will include suggested food combinations and slicing and marinating techniques. You can then get creative, applying these principles and techniques in exciting and innumerable ways.

The recipes in this book are a sacred beginning to a divine holistic living way of life. These recipes will set the pace for an entirely new way of "LIFE"—live life food preparation. It is the intent of the Kwatamani Family Community to teach you how to innercourse with live foods instead of giving you a large quantity of bland recipes that we no longer use. These dishes are primary dishes with the Kwatamani Royal Family. These are traditional Kwatamani recipes.

Some basic equipment:

- *Sharp, stainless steel knives*

- *Garlic press*

Used to press garlic cloves. Avoid the cheap plastic varieties. Look for the sturdy stainless steel ones. Pressing the garlic improves its taste and digestibility.

- *Food Processor*

We recommend the Cuisinart. The food processor can be used for grinding nuts and making puddings, cakes, pie crusts and purees.

Breakfast Treats

Carob Banana Pudding

Ingredients:

bananas
raw carob power
cinnamon
pecans
coconuts

Blend bananas, carob, cinnamon and pecans in food processor with S-blade until smooth. Bust coconut. Pour off coconut water and save. (You can drink it). Remove hard coconut meat from shell. Rinse coconut meat and slice into small chunks. Juice coconut meat. Add the coconut chaff/shavings (left from juicing) to the banana mixture and blend in food processor until smooth or to desired consistency. Place pudding mixture into serving bowls. Add coconut milk to taste.

This recipe is a breakfast/early-day favorite with the Royal Family.

Another breakfast staple....

Organic Raw Oatmeal

Ingredients:

organic oat groats
banana
coconut milk (see Carob Banana Pudding recipe for how to make coconut milk)
medjool dates
cinnamon
fresh-pressed apple juice

Soak oats in apple juice to desired consistency. Remove pits from the dates. Place banana, medjool dates, coconut milk and cinnamon in blender and blend until smooth. Add banana mixture to soaked oats and mix well. Serve. Yummy for live oatmeal!

Note: Please be aware that oat groats are a natural raw and living product of the divine innercourse between the sun and the earth. If you happen to be near or have access to an oat field, then this recipe is ideal. However, if you are depending on your local commercially-oriented health food store, then be prepared to be disappointed to find out that your oat groats will more than likely have been robbed of essential and wholesome vitamins and minerals as well as their active and necessary enzymes all because of somebody's ill-advised idea of instigating heat processing to extend unwholesome shelf-life.

Main dishes

Kush-Hi Supreme

Kush is a dish created by the High Priest Kwatamani over thirty years ago. This dish was made famous as a live foods staple food during the early years of the *First Innercourse*, the first living foods emporium of its kind in America. The dish gained further fame while being served in the *Afrikan Innercourse* and *Old Roots, New Seeds* which was established in Ghana, Liberia, Guinea and Sierra Leone with associated activities in Tanzania, Nigeria and the Ivory Coast. The dish caught on in Asia and Europe during the High Priest Kwatamani's many visits and speaking engagements regarding live foods. This dish is a divinely nourishing dish that is also very filling and tasty.

You begin this dish with the sprouting grain of your choice, preferably quinoa. Quinoa is preferable because of the commercialization, processing and starch content of other grains.

Ingredients:

soaked/sprouted raw quinoa
fresh organic vegetables
onion
scallions
mushrooms
mung bean or soy bean sprouts
carrots
beets
tomatoes
celery
parsley
rosemary
fresh mild chilies (powdered)
basil
extra virgin olive oil
sun evaporated sea water

Rinse 1 c. quinoa. Discard rinsing water. Soak quinoa with spring water until it reaches the desired consistency. Set quinoa aside. Shred 1/2 med. beet and 1 med. carrot. Finely chop remaining vegetables, which should be measured according to your personal likes and desires. Set vegetables aside. Drain off excess water from the quinoa using a strainer. Place quinoa and all vegetables in large mixing bowl. Add herbs and spices to taste. Add 1 T. olive oil. Add sun evaporated sea water to taste. Mix well. Serve. To add that amazing and tantalizing taste to that dish that has made it what it is, kindly prepare a bed of crunchy green leaf lettuce. Romaine is an excellent choice. Break or shred the lettuce well and place around the dish prior to eating. An additional asset to this dish is a nice hot pepper blend.

Live Seed Fou Fou

Ingredients:

pumpkin seeds (presoaked)
sunflower seeds (presoaked)
thyme
basil
green bell pepper
cilantro
fresh pressed garlic
tomato
Thai chili pepper or cayenne
onion
celery
extra virgin olive oil
sun evaporated sea water
lime

Fou fou:

Place seeds in food processor. Add pressed garlic. Add diced onion. (Share garlic proportionately between the fou fou and the soup). Add a small taste of thyme and fresh-squeezed lime juice. Blend until smooth. Remove mixture from food processor. Roll seed mixture into serving-sized balls and set aside.

Soup:

Place all vegetables, hot pepper and remaining spices in blender. Add diced onion. Add pressed garlic. Blend until smooth. Pour mixture into a separate bowl. Add olive oil and sun evaporated sea water to taste. Add fresh-squeezed lime juice to taste. Stir well.

Pour soup over Live Seed Fou Fou to suit taste. Eat.

This dish is best eaten by pinching off bite-sized portions from the fou fou and dipping it in soup. Take your time chewing and savoring this dish. Wow! will be your response to this live seed fou fou.

Brazil Nut Loaf

Ingredients:

brazil nuts (presoaked)
basil
rosemary
garlic
onion
green bell pepper
tomato
celery
extra virgin olive oil
lime
sun evaporated sea water

Place nuts in food processor. Add basil, rosemary and pressed garlic. (Taste your herbs for freshness and flavor. Add in small proportions until you are satisfied. Remember, herbal seasonings create taste, but do not forget that nuts and other food items also have taste. So, be humble to the taste of each ingredient). Process until well mixed, but do not blend until smooth. Dice onion, bell pepper, tomato and celery and place in a large mixing bowl. Add brazil nut mixture to diced vegetables. Add olive oil. Add fresh-squeezed lime and sun evaporated sea water to taste. Mix very well. Serve and eat.

This dish is best served over a nice organic dark green leafy lettuce. What my preference is to take portions of the nut loaf and roll it in the lettuce and add some pepper sauce. My goodness! What a flavorful and nutritious taste! Don't forget to add some vine-ripened tomatoes to your wrap.

Earth and Sea Salad

Ingredients:

wakame
avocado
tomatoes
cucumber
apples
boston lettuce
romaine lettuce
carrots
sweet potato
zucchini
butternut squash
pecans
nori
spinach
olives (please see section on foods for storage and preparation of olives)
arame
lemon
rosemary
thyme
cilantro
extra virgin olive oil

Soak wakame in olive oil. Set aside. Chop the avocado and olives into chunks. Dice tomato, cucumber and apple. Slice lettuces, spinach and cilantro into small slices. Peel sweet potato and butternut squash. Shred carrots, sweet potato, zucchini and butternut squash. Break pecans and nori into small pieces. In a separate jar, with a cover, put olive oil, fresh-squeezed lemon, thyme, rosemary and finely sliced cilantro. Tightly close lid and shake the contents of the jar until well mixed. Set aside. Place all vegetables into a large bowl, add all of the seaweeds (wakame, nori, arame) and the pecans. Mix together well. Place the mixture in your serving bowl and dress with the olive oil herb mixture as desired. Now, it's ready to eat.

Vegetable Dishes

The Original Sproutghetti

This is a 25-year-old recipe from the High Priest Kwatamani

Ingredients:

mung bean or soy bean sprouts
raw apple cider vinegar
tomato
onion
oregano
sage
basil
thyme
garlic
almonds
sun evaporated sea water
lime
bell pepper
mushrooms
olive oil

Start by soaking sprouts in vinegar and sun evaporated sea water. (Please bear in mind that this is a very important preparation technique for creating the special texture of this dish). Put aside. Then, mix olive oil, lime and sun evaporated sea water to taste in large bowl. Stir well. Wash mushrooms thoroughly to remove all dirt. Gently remove stems, taking care not to break the mushroom heads. Place mushroom heads and stems in olive oil mixture. Stir well. Set aside and allow mushrooms to marinate. Place tomatoes, onion, oregano, sage, basil, thyme and garlic in blender and blend until smooth. Place the almonds in food processor and grind into a nut butter. Drain sprouts. Place sprouts in a deep mixing bowl. Add blended tomato sauce to nut butter mixture in food processor. Add fresh-squeezed lime and sun evaporated sea water to tomato/nut mixture to taste. Blend well. Remove mushroom heads and stems from marinade. Add to sprouts. Pour blended mixture over sprouts and mushrooms. Mix by gently turning over sprouts. Eat.

(For proportions: Per 2 c. of sprouts, use one tomato, one medium-sized onion, 3-5 leaves of oregano, 2 leaves of sage, 2-3 leaves of basil, 2-3 leaves of thyme, 1 clove garlic, 1 c. almonds, 1 c. mushrooms, 1/2 small bell pepper).

Cabbage Stir Raw

Ingredients:

cabbage
onions
tomatoes
bell pepper
garlic
extra virgin olive oil
lime
sun evaporated sea water

Slice cabbage into very thin slices. Place into a large mixing bowl. Thinly slice onions and tomatoes. Add onions and tomatoes to cabbage. Add pressed garlic. Add olive oil to taste. Add fresh-squeezed lime juice and sun evaporated sea water to taste. Stir well and eat.

This is a very delicious, yet very simple dish. Therefore, I suggest that you prepare it based upon your desire to eat and the eating desires of those around you. If it were the I in I, preparing a meal for the I in I, I would use 1/2 of a cabbage, 1 tomato, 1 med. bell pepper, 1 med. onion and at least one full clove of garlic. I love garlic! I would add one ounce of olive oil and the juice of half of a lime).

Okra

Ingredients:

okra
tomato
onion
garlic
lime
extra virgin olive oil
sun evaporated sea water

Wash vegetables. Slice okra into very thin rounds and place in mixing bowl. Finely chop tomato and onion. Add to okra. Press garlic. Add pressed garlic to vegetables. Add olive oil. Add fresh-squeezed lime juice and sun evaporated sea water to taste. Stir well. Serve and eat.

This dish is pretty simple. Again, measure your stomach and mix your vegetables according to your flavor-tasting desires for that day.

Broccoli Cauliflower Supreme

Ingredients:

broccoli
cauliflower
onion
garlic
tomato
celery
extra virgin olive oil
lime
basil
thyme
sun evaporated sea water

Wash vegetables. Very finely chop broccoli and cauliflower. Place in large mixing bowl. Thinly slice onion, celery and tomato. Add to broccoli/cauliflower mixture. Add pressed garlic. Add olive oil. Add fresh-squeezed lime juice. Finely slice basil. Add basil, thyme and sun evaporated sea water to taste. Stir all ingredients well. Serve and eat.

Regarding proportions is to take 1/4 medium sized head of broccoli and 1/4 of a medium sized head of cauliflower. Trim to the stems. The proportions of the remaining vegetables are your choice, but do not be afraid of the tomatoes or the seasonings. For example, for this serving size I would use a minimum of 1/2 tomato, 1/2 clove garlic and approximately 1/3 stalk of celery, a few leaves of basil, the leaves of a small sprig of thyme and just a dash of salt, because the celery supplies natural sodium.

Stuffed Mushrooms

Ingredients:

mushrooms
extra virgin olive oil
sun evaporated sea water
lime
oregano
red and green bell pepper
scallion
onion
tomato
red leaf lettuce
celery
cilantro
spinach
garlic

Mix olive oil, sun evaporated sea water, lime and oregano in large bowl. Stir well. Wash mushrooms thoroughly to remove all dirt. Gently remove stems, taking care not to break the mushroom heads. Place mushroom heads and stems in olive oil mixture. Stir well. Set aside, and allow mushrooms to marinate. Finely chop the remaining vegetables and the herbs, placing them in a separate bowl. Add pressed garlic to vegetable/herb mixture. Remove mushroom heads and stems from marinade, and place them in a separate bowl. Pour the marinade sauce over the vegetables and mix well. Stuff mushrooms with the vegetable mixture. (The marinated stems can be eaten by themselves and/or with any remaining vegetables). Serve and eat.

Regarding proportions, the amount of vegetables prepared will be the amount that will fit into the mushrooms.

Onion New-Dos

Ingredients:

onions
tomato
scallion
garlic
extra virgin olive oil
lime
sun evaporated sea water

Thinly slice onions, tomatoes and scallions and place in mixing bowl. Add pressed garlic. Add olive oil, fresh-squeezed lime and sun evaporated sea water to taste. Allow to marinate for a few minutes. Serve and eat.

Spinach

Ingredients:

spinach
parsley
tomato
onion
mushroom
garlic
lime
extra virgin olive oil
sun evaporated sea water

Wash vegetables. Finely chop all vegetables placing them in a large mixing bowl. Add pressed garlic. Add fresh-squeezed lime, olive oil and sun evaporated sea water to taste. Stir well and eat.

Plantains

Ingredients:

plantains
onions
scallions
garlic
rosemary
extra virgin olive oil
lime
sun evaporated sea water

Thinly slice one whole, black, ripe plantain into rounds. Place in mixing bowl. Finely slice 1/4 med. onion and one scallion (using green part only. If the scallion has a developed bud, use the entire scallion and leave out the 1/4 onion). Add to plantains. Add 1 or 2 finely sliced leaves of rosemary. Add 1/4 clove of pressed garlic. Add 1/2 T. olive oil. Add 1 t. of fresh-squeezed lime juice and a pinch of sun evaporated sea water.

This is one of our African and Asian delicacies that changed many a taste bud to eating raw plantains.

Collard Greens

Ingredients:

collard greens
tomato
onions
garlic
extra virgin olive oil
lime
sun evaporated sea water

Very, very, thinly slice 1/4 bunch collard greens, and place in mixing bowl. Thinly slice 1/2 tomato and one small onion. Add to collard greens. Add 1 clove of pressed garlic. Remember, I love garlic. It keeps evil spirits away. Add 1 T. olive oil. Add the juice of 1 small lime. Add sun evaporated sea water to taste. Stir very well and eat. If you really want to enhance the flavor of this dish, please add pepper. I guarantee you that you will truly know what is meant by live, divine soul food.

Mushroom sauce-sage supreme

Ingredients:

mushroom
onions
green bell pepper
plum tomato
thyme
sage
garlic
lime
extra virgin olive oil
sun evaporated sea water
green leaf lettuce, or any other favorite variety of lettuce
nori

Dice mushrooms, onions and bell pepper. Place in large mixing bowl. Dice outer, dry portion of tomato. Remove insides and eat them while you work on this surprise-filled dish. Add thinly sliced sage and thyme. Add pressed garlic. Add olive oil, lime and sun evaporated sea water. Mix well. Please remember to slice the sage very well so that its flavor is evenly spread throughout the entire dish. Slice lettuce. Spread sheet of nori flat. Place a few spoons of the vegetable mixture to the left edge of the nori, and spread evenly from top to bottom. Place sliced lettuce alongside vegetables toward the center of the sheet. Fold bottom edge of the nori over top of vegetables. Gather edge of nori and vegetables, being careful to keep the bottom tucked under. Roll tightly into a roll. It's ready to serve. For extra taste, add some of that flavorful Kwatamani pepper sauce.

Proportions: Use a handful of mushrooms to one small tomato. 1 sm. onion, 1/4 med. bell pepper, 3 leaves of sage and the leaves of one sprig of thyme. Use 1 med. clove of garlic. Please don't forget that I love garlic and I do not want evil spirit relationships around me. Use 2 tsp. of olive oil and sun evaporated sea water to taste.

Corn

Ingredients:

corn
tomato
onion
garlic
scotch bonnet pepper
parsley
cilantro
celery
extra virgin olive oil
lime
sun evaporated sea water

Take one stalk of freshly-picked corn and remove from cob. Place in a large mixing bowl. (Please remember that fresh-picked corn only is sugar, and after the corn has sat a while, it begins to change to starch. Starch is an ingredient that your body definitely does not need. Always remember that your body produces its own special body starch from the natural sugars that it intakes). Place remaining vegetables and herbs in blender in balanced proportions. (Please keep in mind that the base of this dish is corn, so please include all other vegetables accordingly). Blend until smooth. Pour mixture over corn. Add 1/2 T. olive oil. Add the juice of 1/4 small/medium lime. Add sun evaporated sea water to taste. Mix well. Serve and eat this East African favorite made into a live Kwatamani treat.

Sesame Seeds Salad

Ingredients:

raw sesame seeds
onion
yellow bell pepper
red bell pepper
green bell pepper
scallion
tomato
extra virgin olive oil
garlic
sun evaporated sea water
lime
red leaf lettuce

Rinse 1/2 c. sesame seeds. Cover them with spring water, and let soak. Set aside. Dice proportionately 1 small onion and 1 small scallion. Place in a large mixing bowl. Dice 1/4 each medium red, green and yellow bell pepper and add to onions. (In this dish, I love bell pepper; therefore, you judge your taste and act accordingly). Add 1 diced med. plum tomato. Set aside. Drain all water from seeds. Add seeds to vegetables. Add 1/2 T. olive oil. Add 1/2 clove pressed garlic. Add sun evaporated sea water and fresh-squeezed lime to taste. Slice lettuce and place on serving plate. Lay sesame seeds over bed of sliced lettuce. Serve and eat.

Pies

In the Kwatamani way of eating, we do not eat dessert. Instead, we have our fruit pies and sweet treats as a meal in and of themselves or prior to our vegetable meals with plenty of digestion time in between.

Sweet Potato Pie

Ingredients:

sweet potatoes
bananas
pecans (presoaked)
medjool dates
nutmeg
cinnamon

Blend sweet potatoes in food processor with S-blade until they are a puree. Add a small pinch of nutmeg and a small pinch of cinnamon. Add bananas and medjool dates. (Use one banana per medium sized sweet potato). Continue to blend until the mixture is a creamy consistency. Remove mixture and set aside. Wash food processor. To make crust: Place pecans and dates in food processor and process until well-mixed. The consistency should be stiff. If you blend too long, the nuts will turn to butter. Remove nut/date mixture and place in serving dish. Use a teaspoon or your hand to smooth the mixture along the base and sides of the serving dish. Pour sweet potato filling into the serving dish. Smooth. Your pie is ready to eat!

CONCLUSION:

It is our hope that you have had an enjoyable journey into the wonderful world of live foods. It is our greatest wish and desire that you have obtained sufficient knowledge, wisdom and understanding regarding live foods as the first divine act and requirement of a holistic living way of life. Additionally, we beg your brain to totally and absolutely and totally and humbly submit to your supreme inner spirit and to reject the external programming source of the Grand Master of Deceit. We beckon your brain to come into divine oneness with the Supreme inner self so as to gain holistic harmony with the Most Supreme Spirit of Love, Righteousness and the Holistic Living Truth About Supreme Love. In other words, we hope, wish and desire the very best for you and your mental, physical and spiritual being. It is quite clear that if your whole existence comes into divine oneness and decides to wish want, hope and activate the very best for you, you will, in fact, urgently and immediately implement into your daily existence a live foods way of life where you consume the whole and sacred foods of the fruits of the Trees of Life. *i.e.* live fruits, vegetables, seeds, nuts and grains.

APPENDIX

Below is a letter from our California distributor:

Gold Mine Natural Food Company™
7805 Arjons Drive Ste B
San Diego, CA 92126
Ph. (858) 537-9830 Fax (858) 695-0811

Dear Customer,

I want you to know that the Nama® Shoyu you have just purchased is from a very exceptional batch. As you know, Nama® Shoyu is unpasteurized, which means the shoyu is still active after bottling. This batch is even more "active" than usual. This is REALLY GOOD!!! But you need to be careful. Please keep it in the refrigerator. And when you open it, please do so slowly, because it may "pfft" like a can of soda that has been shaken.

Thank you for purchasing Ohsawa® Nama® Shoyu. No other soy sauce in America comes close to it in flavor or quality.

To Your Good Health,

Jean M. Richardson
President

MUSO

MUSO CO. LTD
3-7-22 Nishitenma,
Kita-ku, Osaka 530-0047 JAPAN
TEL: 81-6-6316-6011 FAX: 81-6-6316-6016

Date March 23, 2000

To GOLDMINE FOODS

Attn Mr. GARY CUNNINGHAM

Re Exploding can of Nama shoyu

Sender: Kouji Ishitoko

E-mail: Kouji@muso-intl.co.jp

Num. Of page: / (including this page)

Dear Gary

We discussed the exploring can of Nama shoyu with the manufacturer: Yamaki.

As you know this Nama shoyu is unpasteurized which means the yeast in shoyu is still activating after bottling from barrel. This is the advantage of Nama shoyu. Yeast is the most important bacteria to mature shoyu. But on the other side this cause the exploding problem. Yeast takes in glucose and make alcohol and carbonic acid gas. Carbonic acid gas will fill up the can and exploded.

To solve this problem, major shoyu manufacturer such as Marukin use micro filter for Nama shoyu. Micro filter net size is 0.2 micron and Yeast size sis about 0.5 micron so the yeast will be filtered. Some of amino acid will be also filtered our by micro net, which worsens the taste, aroma and nutrition. Therefore Yamaki never use this method of filtering by micro net. And it has not invented valve like the one usied unpasterurized miso which gets out of carbonic acid gas from can so far.

The only solution at the moment is to store Nama shoyu under 15°C because the most activating temperature for yeast is 20°C to 30°C. But we ship this Nama shoyu with dry container and the inside container get to 30°C even in winter.

We will keep discussing with the manufacturer and try to find the solution.

Best regards,

Kouji Ishitoko

ABOUT THE AUTHOR

This author was born upon the planet in 1946 and, through very many undeclared ways and means, spent the majority of his youthful life consuming a basic live foods diet of fruits, vegetables and nuts. The reactions of his parents, at a young age, were the only basic interference to his maintaining a way of eating and living that came very naturally to him. At an early age, this author received a tremendous amount of conflict as well as found himself very ill after being forced to consume the unwholesome foods of death and devitalization. On several occasions, this author was rescued from the claws of death by his grandmother, who provided wholesome live fruits, vegetables, seeds and nuts for his consumption. This imbalanced relationship occurred into and through the earlier days of his life where he served in the Air Force and found himself struggling with an entire institution bent on forcing him to consume the foods of death. In the late sixties, this author began an amazing turn that led him to a whole, live foods diet. In the late seventies, the author finally got a declaration from his female mate and one of his closest brothers, to begin the emergence of a divine live foods family community. During these times, Sister Iya and Brother Aris joined forces with the echoing spirit of Kwatamani in a journey into a divine and sacred way of life moved into another phase. The High Priest Kwatamani has maintained a live foods diet through the most turbulent times, under the most turbulent conditions, in the most turbulent places.

This most conscious spirit of a man declared more than forty-five years ago that the gathering time would occur in 1999. He has continued to echo this through the ages and now it is coming to pass. And now 1999 has come to pass on the gathering time. The High Priest Kwatamani is most dedicated and most seriously committed to the divine ideology of gathering the Sacred Few. It is the spirit of the Most Supreme Spirit of Love, Righteousness and the Holistic Living Truth About Supreme Love that has continued to spearhead the life of this author. Throughout his travels in North America, South America, the Caribbean, Europe, Asia and Africa and back to North America, his theme has been the same. In order to perpetuate the supreme spirit of life, you must be a consumer of the supreme foods of life, because you are what you eat. And what you put in is what will come out and what comes out is what will come back to you. At this point in time in this lifetime of the High Priest Kwatamani, there are very few who know him or who have knowledge of him that can say that they doubt his most sacred missions and tasks. He is truly a declaration of divine intervention at work. Live and in living color.   It is our hope that you will have the divine privilege of comprehending his most sacred spirit as you take a most humble and most sincere journey through any of his works, especially this book which addresses live foods as the first divine act and requirement of a holistic living way of life.

The Author of this book, High Priest Kwatamani,
Supreme Spiritual Leader of the Kwatamani Family Community:
Supreme Ancestral Soothsayer, Soul Seer and Spiritual Healer

Kwa-She-I-Ta, the ancestral daughter spirit
who emerged upon the seen January 29, 1999,
the Sacred Spirit and the earthly symbol of "The Gathering Time"
and the anointing energy of livefoodsunchild.com

2739244